College Football's Conference Warfare

By Steven Donohue

To my grandfather,
Who taught me what first down meant—SMD

Table of Contents

Rules

In the beginning, God created light, and the planets, and eventually man. Later, man created football, though that was more difficult. Legend holds that Rutgers College and the College of New Jersey (now Princeton University) played the first game of football on November 6, 1869. Something was certainly played that day in New Brunswick, and the game was called "foot ball" by spectators, but we likely would not recognize the sport if we stumbled upon the scrimmage. Each side could field 25 men at a time (Princeton played with only 23). Players could not carry the ball, but instead kicked and slapped it towards their goal. Teams scored points only by kicking the ball through parallel posts at the ends of the field. Rutgers won the first proto-football game 6–4; the schools played again one week later, with Princeton winning that contest 8–0. Those were the only two games in 1869, so the two New Jersey teams split the mythical national championship that year. Unfortunately for Scarlet Knights fans, Rutgers has never won another.

The game swept quickly across the Northeast, enthralling students at Harvard and Yale in particular. During those formative years, there was not one game of football, but several, each a variation on a melody that had never been clearly established. After about a decade, players were permitted to carry the ball, turning football into something more like rugby than soccer. Eleven players on the field became standard. Scoring was altered to allow points either by kicking the ball through posts or by carrying the ball to the edge of the opponent's territory. Football in 1870 was not football in 1880, which in turn was not football in 1890.

Perhaps the only constant throughout those early years was the game's palpable brutality. Coaches stressed strength, not strategy. Rather than spreading players across the pitch, teams collided in the middle of the field, slogging their way inch by hard-earned inch through their opponent's territory. Punts were common, and points were rare; two scores were usually sufficient to win a contest. Teams deliberately wore one another down over the course of the seventy-minute struggle like fighters in a boxing match, seizing upon their foe's injury and fatigue to gain miniscule advantages.

Two risky tactics exacerbated the frequent injuries. The first of those tactics, the infamous flying wedge, called for the largest players on offense to line up several yards behind the line of scrimmage in a V shape, with the junction pointing towards the opposite team. Before the snap, these behemoths sprinted towards their opponent. The running back received the ball at the snap, and then attempted to stay inside the wedge as his linemen charged ahead. Defenders, hoping to penetrate the wall of players protecting the ball carrier, charged towards the sprinting wedge, guaranteeing carnage for both sides. Coaches decried the wedge while using it liberally; it was too successful to disappear of its own accord. Soon the maneuver became synonymous with the sport's recklessness.

Harvard had invented the wedge play in 1892. Two years later, it was banned. For all the flying wedge's notoriety, teams prohibited this strategy before it could cause any real damage. Wedge-like maneuvers still existed, and coaches often pushed the boundaries of the line as far as possible, but the wedge itself has earned too large a place in history as a villain of the sport.

Although coaches banned the wedge maneuver, the second dangerous tactic, "mass play," remained common. At the conclusion of the down, teammates would force a small running back to remain on his feet as bulkier linemen pushed through the opposition. In this strategy, the ball carrier was less a football player than the unlucky vessel by which his team transported the ball into enemy territory. In one particularly dangerous variant of this mass play, the running back was thrown by a teammate over the pile of bodies amassed in the field's center, earning a few extra feet at the expense of the running back's health.

The rules created a violent enough sport, but the natural aggressiveness of the players compounded problems further still. Runners turned their backs and threw themselves into contact, exposing their spines and skulls to danger in return for a few inches worth of momentum. No pre-snap neutral zone yet existed, so any players not charging the other side before the snap began the play as close to their opponents as possible. In that heated environment, fistfights and brawls were frequent. Linemen intentionally poked one another's eyes violently enough to cause bleeding. Tacklers targeted their opponents' heads in an era when competitors ridiculed helmet use as unmanly. Because teams could not substitute injured players without losing their services for the game, injuries worsened as the contest wore on, leading to permanent damage or, sometimes, death.

A great deal of mythology has developed surrounding the eradication of violence from football. The most commonly told tale is that, as college football degenerated into wanton thuggery, the public demanded that either changes be made, or—without those changes—that football be eliminated from campuses. At some point, so the myth goes, the din grew so loud that President Theodore Roosevelt stepped in, called football coaches from around the country to the White House, and threatened the representatives with the sport's abolition if football could not be made less violent. Frightened to action, the coaches curtailed violence and saved football from itself.

As with many myths, there is some truth to the story. Roosevelt did call together representatives from several leading colleges in the summer of 1905 to discuss football's safety issues. This was a common tactic for Roosevelt, who believed that many problems could be solved through gathering the parties to the disagreement and applying the force of his will. The chief executive was an avid football fan and vigorously opposed those who wanted to abolish the sport. Roosevelt believed America was in danger of losing the rugged virtues that had propelled the settlers to conquer the now-tamed western frontier, and that the clamor over football's safety was another sign of the country's modern effeminacy.

Yet Roosevelt was also concerned that his son, who was soon to begin playing football for the Harvard freshman team, might be in danger. Football forged tougher men, and Roosevelt understood that injuries were bound to happen (indeed, Teddy Jr. broke his nose that year during a game). Although the president would not entertain notions that football was inherently too dangerous a sport for a civilized nation, as others had claimed, Roosevelt believed that the roughest edges could at least be smoothened. The coaches who attended the meeting left with a genuine appreciation for the need to reform the game.

But the media firestorm over football's epidemic of injures did not ignite until *after* Roosevelt called his meeting. Football's safety had long been a lingering issue, mentioned from time to time in newspaper editorials and by concerned academics, but never enough to slow the sport's growing popularity. Before 1905, no more than a handful of vociferous dissenters argued that football should be abolished.

Yet by drawing attention to the issue, President Roosevelt gave the newspapers of the yellow journalism era a new topic to sensationalize, and the meeting on safety primed the public for evidence of football's brutality. A couple dozen individuals died playing football each year, with a few of these deaths occurring in college and the remainder in the various semi-professional leagues scattered across the country. Both the seasons before and after Roosevelt's summit were mostly normal—a few deaths here and there, but in line with what usually had been the case.

The facts had not changed, but the lens through which those facts were perceived had been altered, or perhaps cleared. With Roosevelt's recognition of safety in football as worthy of presidential awareness, each fatality garnered attention well beyond what might have been expected even a season or two before. Especially jarring was the death of Harold Moore, a Union College player accidentally kicked in the head by his own teammate in a match against NYU. Although Moore was one of only three college players who died in 1905—roughly on par with previous seasons—the combination of a now-crusading public and a highly publicized death in the nation's largest city proved explosive. Cries for reform or outright abolition rang out across the country, as newspaper readers increasingly associated college football with bloodsport unbecoming of America's youth. Columbia University banned the game within days of the tragedy.

The men who controlled football were sympathetic to the idea that reform was needed—they had been sympathetic since Roosevelt's summit, if not before. Yet changing football proved difficult. Many of the people being asked (or forced) to alter the game were responsible for its wild success. Their sport was almost uniquely popular, second only to baseball amongst team sports in media attention and popular participation.

Foremost among those founders was Walter Camp, the legendary Yale coach who had nearly single-handedly created the sport as it then existed. Camp transformed football from pseudo-soccer into something distinctive, and at the same time turned Yale into a powerhouse that dominated college football for decades. Those fathers of modern football, including Camp, came mostly from schools that disproportionately benefitted from rough-and-tumble mass play. Demanding that football's forefathers abandon their creation was a great deal to ask of them, and there was no guarantee that the new football would be any more successful than New Coke.

Not all coaches were wedded to the old style of play. As football spread from the Northeast to the heartland, different approaches predominated in different locations. In the Midwest, for example, coaches Amos Alonzo Stagg at the University of

Chicago and Fielding Yost at Michigan pioneered a more wide-open, briskly paced style of play, favoring speed over size. Although an oversimplification, Northeastern football was one-dimensional, almost literally. Players advanced the football along a line at the center of the field, and resistance was met with brute strength. Yost and Stagg took the game to two dimensions—the ball could be moved *around* the opponent more easily than through the opponent. The line became a plane, with Yost and Stagg overcoming their disadvantage in size through speed.

Unsatisfied stopping at two dimensions, coaches such as Stagg and Yost hoped to open up play still further through use of the experimental forward pass. The Midwestern coaches hoped that a move towards an aerial game would prevent injuries, since mass play would no longer be advantageous. They also believed the three-dimensional game would favor the style of play they had perfected in two dimensions.

On the other hand, many Northeastern coaches believed, not irrationally, that their rivals were using the safety issue as a Trojan horse for undercutting the Northeastern schools' supremacy. Football with passing was fundamentally different than the game then being played. Many coaches doubted whether success in one version of football would carry over to the new, supposedly improved version. Yet even those coaches understood that some changes were necessary, if only to divert the attacks launched by safety-minded critics. The status quo was no longer tenable.

***

Altering the rules was a more complicated affair in 1905 than it had been in the 1880s. When the early game was evolving from primordial chaos, only a few schools along the east coast played football. Most of the sport's founding fathers communicated with one another often, and changing the game created few logistical problems. Half a dozen coaches would agree that some rule wasn't quite working, they would tweak that rule, and the game would be different the following year.

But football in 1905 was played not only in Princeton and New Haven, but also Ann Arbor and Chicago, Lincoln and Norman, even Berkeley and Palo Alto. All schools (mostly) followed the same rulebook, yet the Midwestern and Western games looked far different from the Northeastern game. Camp at Yale created piles of bodies on the middle of the field; Yost at Michigan ran around those piles. If Pandora's Box were opened by calling a constitutional convention on the rules of football, the nation could fracture into several different factions, each playing a variant of football incompatible with the others. This process had already begun in the Golden State, where Stanford and Cal replaced their annual football game with rugby over safety concerns. Whatever rules changes agreed upon would need to be compromise measures amenable to all.

Charged with creating the authoritative national rulebook was the newly established Inter Collegiate Athletic Association ("ICAA"), an informal committee of football coaches and other influential figures within the sport. Despite the overrepresentation of Northeastern schools such as Yale and Harvard, the ICAA recognized that unpopular practices like mass play needed to end. Northeasterners, such as Yale's Walter Camp, may have dreamt of maintaining their advantage by retaining mass play, but those men also wanted to keep football a national pastime. Camp and the others were ambitious and competitive men, but they also knew their legacies rested primarily on their creation of the sport, and not the transient success of their programs.

Foremost amongst the rule changes was the introduction of the forward pass. The rules governing the passing game were not handed down on Sinai, fully formed and sacrosanct. Instead, coaches across the country experimented in their scrimmages, mixing and matching combinations to determine what rules would best suit their needs. Should an incomplete pass result in a turnover at the place where the ball landed, or a turnover at the original line of scrimmage, or merely a loss of down? How many and which players are eligible to catch passes? Is there any minimum or maximum number of yards a pass may travel? Can multiple forward passes be made behind the original line of scrimmage? There was no obvious answer to any of those questions, and each one was debated and argued at length.

Harold Moore's death inaugurated a process that stretched over several years as coaches experimented with proposed rules. A gradual, evolutionary process weeded out rules unpopular to both coaches and the public. At first, only two players were eligible to receive passes; this expanded little by little until six offensive players could do so. The field was originally divided both vertically and horizontally, and legal passes had to travel laterally and downfield; this was soon abandoned as the "checkerboard" field was replaced with the gridiron. An incomplete pass resulted in an immediate change of possession, not merely the end of the play. The ball was larger and more spherical than the modern football, not too different from a basketball, making passing more difficult. Amendments and reforms continue to this day, of course, but never again would football face a rules crisis as it did at the beginning of the 20th century. The sport borne from the maelstrom looked much like our modern sport in most respects. All changes since have been mere fiddling with the details.

The ICAA was as successful as it possibly could have been under the circumstances. The public uproar over player safety almost immediately dulled to the tolerable whisper that had rumbled before the 1905 crisis. The national rulebook also successfully standardized the sport. Even schools and regions that were unrepresented at the original ICAA conference found the new rules agreeable. When Cal and Stanford renewed their football rivalry after a decade of playing rugby, the ICAA platform was an obvious disembarking point, since adopting those rules allowed the California schools to play Northeastern and Midwestern colleges as well. As western and southern schools adopted the new rulebook and participated in later rules modifications, the ICAA was renamed the National Collegiate

Athletic Association ("NCAA") reflecting the group's expanding geographic scope.

Unfortunately, although the fury over player welfare ignited the revolution, the new rulebook did not make football much safer. A few players each season—about as many as prior to 1905—died on the football field in the years following the changes. Improving safety equipment, and changing attitudes about wearing that equipment, prevented far more gridiron fatalities than the introduction of the forward pass or the discouragement of mass play.

Yet, just as Roosevelt's summit—and not the facts on the field—had launched the crisis, the rules changes mostly extinguished the public's safety concerns despite not doing much to improve player safety. Perhaps the violence of a world war blunted American attitudes towards mortality. Perhaps a lack of urging from prominent public figures such as President Roosevelt dimmed the issue. Perhaps the sport became so popular after the rule changes opened up play that fans better tolerated a small number of deaths each season.

***

Or perhaps another question captured the public consciousness and crowded out the safety worries. In hindsight, concerns over the well-being of the players were probably destined to sort themselves out. Advances in technology would dampen the problem, and even if some coaches favored riskier styles, no one was pro-death or pro-injury. The introduction (and requirement) of leather helmets alone probably saved several lives and prevented innumerable head injuries each season. If football could be played without maiming its competitors—an open question, perhaps—all were determined to see it happen, and ingenious inventors and engineers stood to profit if they could arrive at the solution.

Football's safety crisis attracted President Roosevelt's bully pulpit, but a broad range of "academic" issues raised the public's ire for far longer. Even if football should be played, why must it be played by college students? Why should universities pour their scarce resources into a game? The most satisfying answers were also the least convincing. Coaches and sympathetic administrators justified football as a needed physical complement to the academic experience of its students. Properly developed men needed strong bodies and stout leadership to go along with sharp minds. Football cultivated the martial qualities in ways the classroom could not.

So did many other sports, however, without the omnipresent specter of death and mutilation. Football might contribute marginally to the health of the student body, but if this was the only benefit, the cure was surely worse than the disease. At a minimum, football was not *essential* to adolescent development, and the uproar over player safety made implausible the claims that abandoning the game would endanger student fitness. The health argument for college football was a wash (at best), with the game taking in lacerations, concussions, and death more than what it gave in fitness and "manliness." If fitness were the main concern, why not promote track and field over football? Besides, the track team did not threaten the solvency of athletic departments as football did. Nor did track spawn the win-at-all-costs attitude that spread like plague from school to school.

Still worse, football players often learned little in college except football. Rarely did players satisfy the formal entrance requirements of their schools. All too frequently, players did not even attend class, ditching coursework in autumn during the college football season and roaming the countryside in the spring for professional gigs. When the players actually attended class, teachers expected little from them. Athletes were shepherded into easy courses designed to maximize their time on the practice field. Administrators rearranged class schedules for the entire university to better meet the needs of football coaches. Supportive professors taught classes to athletes segregated from the remainder of the

university; these courses were given impressive titles to ɩ
true nature as busywork.

Tied up with the idea of athlete-as-student was the equally
robust idea that the athlete should also be an amateur,
representing his school only for the privilege of doing so.
Academics (attending class) and amateurism (playing for free) do
not have to be linked. Conceptually, you can combine the ideas
any which way. Students taking vigorous courses can be
reimbursed for their football contributions; or, real students can
play as amateurs; or, colleges could license out their football team
to paid professionals with no connection to the school beyond the
logo.

But fans of that era saw amateurism problems and academic
problems as largely the same issue. Football players, the public
thought, should represent the school as other students represent
the school. The proper student, by definition, attends class. He
also goes about his extracurricular activities only for the self-
satisfaction of doing so, and if he were unwilling to play without
pay, other students — real students — would gladly do so. In other
words, amateurism was, at heart, the belief that a college football
team should be made up of students who happen to attend a
particular school. Princeton and Rutgers had not recruited its
teams in 1869; the players simply showed up, fresh from Latin and
biology class. Reimbursement for performance is ridiculous within
this mental framework, in the same way that reimbursing students
who join French club or academic bowl in high school strikes us as
absurd.

This "amateur code" of college football has always been a
slippery concept, open to interpretation and reasonable debate.
But whatever the exact boundaries of the amateur code, many
schools stretched the concept beyond recognition. One strategy,
popular with schools in the Midwest, was to provide athletes with
jobs, then overcompensate the athletes for their work. Often, these

"jobs" were merely ghost-payroll fronts used to funnel money to players, with no work required whatsoever.

Scholarships were another point of contention. Pure athletic scholarships were frowned upon in that era, looking too much like pay for performance. Even academic scholarships that happened to be given to athletes looked somewhat fishy, though these were allowed. After all, it was not fair to exclude athletes from money that was available to every other student at the school.

Because the public frowned upon scholarships for athletic contributions, recruiting became an exercise in not saying things while remaining perfectly clear. A coach could not offer financial support to a high school athlete. He could mention, however, all the fantastic opportunities that awaited those who enroll at the university, while highlighting the numerous academic scholarships for those that qualify.

Coaches maintained plausible deniability by using boosters — outsiders that supported the program — to do the truly dirty work. Fans might drop off an envelope with money at the household of a recruit or player with no prompting from the school whatsoever. Local restaurants fed players for free. Other students completed coursework for athletes.

Identifying undue influence or shady practices could be practically impossible. Family and friends would be expected to weigh in on the important decision of where a youngster attends college. Yet what about when the roles of booster and friend intersected? How much of a fan can someone be before influencing an athlete to attend a certain school becomes improper? And if untraceable cash were involved at any point in the process, no one but the giver and the recipient would have any knowledge of it.

Like the rules governing the game on the field, regional attitudes and preferences towards the amorphous "amateur code" evolved. Unlike the on-the-field rules, however, it was not essential for all schools that competed against one another to adopt *exactly* the same regulations concerning amateur play. When two football teams meet, they must absolutely agree to the size of the field, the shape of the ball, and so on—one team cannot play on a 120-yard field while the other uses a 100-yard field. A national rulebook, such as that created by the NCAA, simplifies this process, and going outside of that rulebook makes finding competition more difficult for the dissenting team.

But if two schools adhere to different amateur or academic standards, they can still play a game of football against one another, though one team may be at a disadvantage. An official national "amateur code" was not essential. If one team strayed too far from the rest—outright maintaining a payroll for players, perhaps—the others might respond by boycotting that team until it more closely adhered to the group's standards. Programs needed only to stay near enough to the amateur code (whatever it might be) that other schools would continue to play them.

***

One early effort to regulate the recruiting process began in 1895, when representatives from eight Midwestern colleges met in Chicago to discuss how to cleanse the unsavory atmosphere that had already developed. The octet agreed not to provide athletic scholarships, with each school finding that direct aid for football performance violated their notion of the amateur code. Yet, on the principle that players should not be disadvantaged compared to other students, the schools permitted one another to provide athletes with academic scholarships, provided that the athletes could demonstrate their academic ability. Athletes could also earn their tuition by working side jobs, just as any other student might, and schools could help the athletes find those jobs. The agreement was certainly not the only possible "amateur code"—one could imagine something stricter or more permissive—but the schools were at least attempting to regularize standards. Before the end of the decade, Iowa and Indiana joined their counterparts at Illinois, Minnesota, Wisconsin, Purdue, Michigan, Northwestern, and the

University of Chicago to create what they called Western Conference. After the addition of Ohio State in 1912 and the readmission of Michigan in 1917 following a nine-year hiatus, the alignment became known as the Big Ten.

Athletic conferences sprouted around the country. The benefits of the conference were obvious, even apart from the establishment of consistent rules regarding amateurism. Rivalries across schools developed from repeated competition; these rivalries meant heightened fan passions, which in turn meant higher ticket prices and more revenue. Scheduling games became easier: no longer would schools have to resort to playing dental colleges and squads from military bases to complete their season. Because travel before the age of interstate highways and commercial aviation was difficult, each of these conferences was regional, usually spanning only a few states and a couple of hundred miles at their most distant points.

Unsurprisingly, schools often ignored the conference amateurism rules. Money in college athletics, as in politics, is like water on pavement—destined to find the cracks. The Big Ten briefly kicked out Iowa for violating recruiting rules in 1907; Hawkeyes representatives claimed their school was a scapegoat for violations occurring throughout the conference. The Big Ten schools were no guiltier for having written down their rules and failed to abide by them, but they were no more innocent for merely having written rules either. Conference arrangements alone did little to strengthen the amateur code.

Just as the Roosevelt summit fastened the public attention on safety in college football, an outside influence stimulated interest in a topic that had been simmering for decades. The Carnegie Institution—a non-profit group established through seed money by steel tycoon Andrew Carnegie and dedicated to solving national problems of all varieties—set out in the mid-1920s to document the state of college athletics. Investigators crisscrossed the country, recording both anecdotes and more substantive data on almost every aspect of college sports. The Institution published its exhaustive report in 1929, covering everything from player hygiene to the effect of athletic schedules on study habits.

No section of the report received more attention than that on amateurism and recruiting. Not much had changed since the Big Ten was created over thirty years before; if anything, football's increasing popularity had made problems worse. The report implicated nearly every major college football program, estimating that 75 percent of the schools in the nation were illicitly paying their players. Most of the honest programs were perennial losers.

Probably only a few hundred people read the lengthy report in full, but newspapers across the country trumpeted the juicier findings. Players accepting illegal benefits! Athletes not attending class! Just as during the safety crisis, none of the underlying facts had changed; all these problems had existed for decades (interestingly, sections of the report discussing injuries and substandard medical care for college athletes—a topic that had provoked such feverish debate only two decades earlier—went virtually unnoticed). Once again, as if on cue, editorial pages throughout the nation called for reform or, in the case of a few radical outliers, abolition of college football.

The reaction to the report foreshadowed the impending disaster, but the initial outburst quickly dissipated. In an example of particularly unfortunate timing, the Carnegie Institution released its report only one week before the Black Tuesday stock market crash of 1929, and public attention understandably drifted away from football and towards weightier issues. Apart from distracting the public, the Great Depression also temporarily relieved the problem, as formerly cash-flushed boosters could no longer bestow lavish gifts upon their favored programs. With less money floating around the college football marketplace, schools could no longer engage in the worst of the excesses documented in the report.

Depression also undercut the status quo in another way. The forerunning Big Ten guidelines created a nationwide expectation for other schools to follow. Southern schools resisted the nationalization of the Big Ten's rules, which tolerated job assistance but prohibited schools from providing athletic scholarships. Finding make-work jobs for athletes in the post-Reconstruction South was a struggle even before the bottom fell out of the stock market; the Great Depression made these efforts futile. Nor were academic scholarships much of a solution; southern elementary and secondary schools lagged behind their northern counterparts, and athletes recruited from the South often had difficulty demonstrating academic merit.

The Rubicon was finally crossed in 1935, when the Southeastern Conference ("SEC") became the first major conference to authorize athletic scholarships. The façade had fallen. If players were going to be compensated, the SEC reasoned, the most direct route was as good as any other.

Not all schools accepted this logic. To the northern schools, athletic scholarships were the fatal last step from which amateurism could never return. Ordinary students could earn scholarships for their academic merit. Ordinary students could work in the offseason to pay their bills. But ordinary students were not given free rides at the university merely to play games. Northern programs distrusted those in the south, believing they acted from self-interest and nothing more; southern programs believed the same in return. Sectional rivalry alone would have been perfectly healthy, but rivalry had turned to disunion. If the regions believed they could not fairly compete with the others, they simply would not try. College football as a national sport would be lost, disintegrating into separate fiefdoms across the nation.

Fashioning a national plan would be difficult though. If too strict, some schools would refuse to comply and college football could fracture into different leagues, just as if one set of schools chose to play on a 150-yard field. If too lenient, the concept of amateur play would forever be gone, and the public—which was still very much invested in the amateur code—would turn away from the game. Even the southern schools, where concern about the amateur code was weakest, were worried that moving too far towards professionalism would endanger college football's popularity.

The northern and southern systems coexisted uneasily for a decade, largely because World War II prevented many schools from fielding competitive teams. The debate over amateurism, however, never vanished, and some programs decided that their conception of amateurism was entirely incompatible with modern college football. One Big Ten school, the University of Chicago—the program of Amos Alonzo Stagg, who had done so much to introduce the forward pass to the game; the program of Jay Berwanger, the first Heisman Trophy winner—disbanded its football program entirely. The school's academic representatives no longer believed the rising cost of fielding a competitive football team was justified by the return on investment.

Football's monetary burdens were overwhelming for small schools such as Chicago. Coaches earned higher salaries, facilities cost more money, and recruits wanted more benefits than ever before. But the psychological costs, not the financial ones, were the impetus for Chicago's abandonment of football. The game was just too dirty, especially now that schools were proudly paying athletes. And so a founding member of the nation's oldest athletic conference played football no more.

***

The NCAA, whose uniform rulebook had settled the safety crisis earlier in the century, offered a compromise amateurism plan in 1946. Their solution, gracelessly named the Sanity Code, allowed teams to pay players' tuition and feed players once a day during the season. Off-campus recruiting, however, was prohibited. Coaches could explain school financial aid policies to recruits, but they could not make any firm offers to provide aid (the line between providing information and offering aid was never clear). Finally, scholarships could only go towards tuition. Teams could not pay for boarding, books, or the other incidental costs of attending college. The Sanity Code provided for only one punishment against those that committed violations: expulsion from the NCAA.

Southern schools were furious. Midwestern schools, after all, could now pay the tuition of its athletes while filling in the Sanity Code's gaps by finding make-believe jobs for players. Meanwhile, the Sanity Code deprived the southern schools of their foremost recruiting tool—the all-expenses-paid athletic scholarship. Jobs were still scarce south of the Mason-Dixon Line, even during the post-World War II boom, and southern businesses certainly did not have room on their payroll for pretend employees. The Sanity Code did nothing to change the underlying reasons that the different regional policies existed in the first place.

Several aggrieved schools launched a frontal assault against the Sanity Code and the NCAA. Fittingly, the school founded by Thomas Jefferson, America's foremost revolutionary rebel, led the charge. But Jefferson's University of Virginia was not alone in mutiny. The "Sinful Seven" schools—Virginia, Villanova, Boston College, The Citadel, Maryland, Virginia Military Institute, and Virginia Polytechnic Institute—openly violated the Sanity Code, proudly continuing under the old recruiting ethos. Echoing the rhetoric of a century before, the schools insisted that they did not want to secede, but the principles at play were more important than NCAA membership.

Many NCAA members, even apart from the Sinful Seven, opposed the Code. Not only might those displeased with the Sanity Code vote against expulsion of the Sinful Seven, but if expulsion were successful, those other dissenters might secede as well. Expulsion was a weapon best used sparingly and against single targets. Removing one school from the NCAA would devastate that school's athletic program, as that school could no longer play other NCAA members. Expelling a group of schools, however, would be the end of the NCAA as a national organization; the NCAA would be punishing *itself* as much as those it expelled.

If the organization did not punish flagrant violators, however, the Sanity Code—or any other rules requiring and regulating amateurism—would be worthless. And if the standards did not apply across the whole nation, the different regions would continue distrusting one another's rules as inadequate.

The NCAA took a vote on expulsion of the Sinful Seven despite the danger of alienating southern schools. Approval of two-thirds of the NCAA membership was needed to expel schools. Although over half the members did vote for expulsion, there was enough opposition from two blocs to stop the measure. The southern schools voted against expulsion as expected, still hoping to reform the NCAA rather than abandon it entirely. An unlikelier source of resistance came from Northeastern schools, which had been so critical in creating the NCAA four decades before. Those schools virulently opposed athletic scholarships, but they also did not want to see their creation abandoned. Rather than participate in the disintegration of the NCAA, the Northeastern schools relented.

With the Sanity Code's de facto castration, the NCAA was left once again with no official policy towards amateurism. This would not do; even in the South, the public still clamored for the cleansing of college football. Over the next decade, under the leadership of Walter Byers, the NCAA adopted policies that were less strict, but more easily enforced. For example, the NCAA caved on the Sinful Seven's demands, allowing athletic scholarships regardless of financial need or academic performance. Schools could now cover tuition, room and board, books, and could even give their players fifteen dollars each month for laundry.

This was a funny sort of amateurism, one quite a journey from the version extolled at the beginning of the century. Then again, that version of amateurism never reflected reality anyway. And there were still limits to the new leniency. Financial aid had to come directly from the school; payouts from boosters were still prohibited. Teams were also forbidden from giving different amounts to different players; the third-string center would earn as much as the star quarterback. Finally, all teams were restricted to the same levels of aid: tuition, boarding, a few dollars in laundry money, but no more.

The NCAA drew the borders of the new amateur code narrowly enough that all schools cared to defend them: a least common denominator amateurism policy. If individual schools or conferences wished to tie their hands with more restrictive policies, then they were free to do so. Some schools did exactly that; Ivy League programs do not provide athletic scholarships for any sport to this day, though generous need-based academic aid packages are often available to Ivy League athletes. Most schools and most conferences, however, took full advantage of the authority granted by the NCAA. What had once been a furtive, semi-questionable practice of giving scholarships solely for athletic ability was now justified as being within the rules.

***

The new, nationalized, stripped-down amateurism standards had one final effect: they increased the NCAA's power and importance well beyond that of a simple rule-making organization. The NCAA now officially had authority to police amateurism violations. Conferences could still mete out their own penalties, but the national organization would have the final word.

Under the old Sanity Code, violations had been clear. The NCAA needed no investigation to uncover the Sinful Seven. Those schools openly flouted the rules and grounded their defense in principle, not in innocence. The Sanity Code was full of bright lines, and it was generally not hard to find out whether a coach had been recruiting off-campus, or whether schools were offering scholarships.

Now, the easiest-to-track aid was permitted, while secret payments—the fifty-dollar handshake, the wink-and-a-nod car loans, the mysterious new apartment with rent well below market value—were forbidden. Uncovering these new offenses required guile and, more importantly, money. Unlike schools, the NCAA does not sell tickets to football games, nor does the faceless agency have boosters to draw upon for donations. The NCAA holds championship tournaments in several sports—the most prominent (and profitable) of which is the annual men's basketball tournament—but most of these events do not even pay for themselves. Each member school also paid the NCAA a small fee each year, but this fee was kept low to encourage membership— only a few hundred dollars per year at the time. Before 1950, the NCAA war chest rarely held much more than $10,000—hardly enough to sustain a single investigation, much less several. The organization needed a new source of revenue to fund the endless investigations necessary under the new amateur code. Fortunately for the NCAA, one was close at hand.

Spreading across eleven hundred acres of Queens, the 1939 New York World's Fair boldly promised the Dawn of a New Day to all who attended. This gaze into the future came at the perfect time, as the present could hardly have been bleaker. The organizers of the New York World's Fair began their work in 1935, six years after the Black Tuesday stock market crash. When the Fair opened in April 1939, war drums and jackboots could be heard faintly from afar; when the Fair concluded in October 1940, Nazi and Soviet armies had ravished Poland, Finland, Norway, Sweden, and France. Throughout America, people sensed that things would get much worse before they improved — why not indulge in a little escapism?

The public, demanding captivation, was not disappointed. The florescent light bulb made its first appearance, ensuring that the World of Tomorrow would be flooded with dim, sterile light. Continental Baking provided samples of its improved and now-sliced Wonder Bread (someday, our futuristic fantasies will appear just as mundane). The versatile fabric nylon, so valuable to both the coming war effort and future male fantasies, was displayed. And on September 30, 1939, fairgoers watched the very first televised football game.

The decision to show Waynesburg College versus Fordham University as the first televised game in history seems peculiar today. No Texas or Oklahoma, Ohio State or Michigan, USC or UCLA, Alabama or Auburn? No *Notre Dame*? Yet this was the golden age of Fordham Rams football, immortalized by the Seven Blocks of Granite that stood across their offensive line in 1936 and 1937 (one of those Blocks — Vince Lombardi — would later coach the Green Bay Packers to victories in the first two Super Bowls). There were also more practical reasons to choose Fordham. Early television networks, like radio stations, could broadcast their programs only over a limited area. Selecting Fordham for the broadcast let New Yorkers at the Fair watch one of their home teams.

Unfortunately, the game was a bore. Fordham brought in Waynesburg, a small private college in Southwest Pennsylvania, as a punching bag to prepare the Rams for bigger matches later that season against Alabama, Pittsburgh, and cross-city nemesis NYU. And although Waynesburg would score the first touchdown in television history, Fordham quickly turned the game into a 34–7 laugher, winning the game and a place in trivia contests forever. The broadcast was obviously threadbare compared to modern productions. There was no instant replay, no helmet-cam, no Goodyear blimp shots, no shirtless fat guys in the audience mugging for the camera. Still, the production was not without its frills. One feature was pre-game interviews with players and coaches, conducted by a young broadcaster named Mel Allen.

The historic event was a catalyst for neither program. Waynesburg College played only one more game in 1939, losing 20–0 to Duquesne University before calling it a season. Fordham finished 1939 with a respectable, though somewhat disappointing, 6–2 record, but two years later, the Fordham sidelined its football program until the end of World War II. They never rekindled the magic, and the Rams won just one game in 1946 and 1947 combined.

Waynesburg's live sacrifice may not have inaugurated the next great era in Fordham football, but the television venture had just begun. The first commercially broadcast college football game came a year later in 1940, when another urban powerhouse, the University of Pennsylvania ("Penn"), trounced the University of Maryland 51–0. Television was still mostly experimental—only a handful of viewers could watch these early broadcasts—but every Penn Quakers home game during the 1940s was televised.

Television and football paired perfectly. The sport was popular in 1940, but America was still a baseball-centric nation, perhaps because a broadcaster could better capture baseball on the radio. An announcer could convey the location of each pitch, the place on the field where the batter hit the ball, and the closeness of the play at first base, all without sacrificing a description of meaningful action elsewhere on the field. By charting the course of the ball, a radio broadcaster could impart almost everything the viewer in the stands was watching.

Football was less amenable to the spoken word. At any given moment, 22 players would be moving somewhere on the field, each serving an important role. As in baseball, there was plenty of down time between plays, but in the few seconds during which action occurred, only a fraction of the details could be described. In what formation did the offense line up? Was there any pre-snap motion? Did any guards pull? Did the wide receivers run routes, or did they block immediately? Which player did the left offensive tackle block? How about the fullback? Which hole did the running back hit? Did the defensive line slant to either side? With television, a viewer at home knew more than merely what a radio announcer managed to convey.

While a godsend to the dedicated fan, there was a downside to television. Since football was so much better seen than heard, football fans before television had to attend games to follow their team actively. Teams invested heavily in massive "bowl" stadiums, dug directly into the ground and often holding a then-unprecedented seventy-thousand patrons. Those ticket sales were needed both to fund less profitable sports and to pay down the debt incurred constructing the stadiums. But why would anyone spend money, fight traffic, and tolerate freezing temperatures when they could stay home and watch the game?

A successful school, such as Penn, could recoup the money lost on ticket sales by selling television networks the right to broadcast their games. By 1950, Penn earned $150,000 a year (or about $1.35 million in 2010 dollars) from the American Broadcasting

Corporation ("ABC") for regional broadcasts of Penn football. The television broadcasts may have cannibalized ticket sales, but as long as college football remained popular, there would remain a market to see successful teams in person. The decline in attendance—at least for teams like Penn—would not be severe.

But not every team was Penn, either on the football field or at the negotiating table. What would the Waynesburgs of the world do when fans started watching Penn in the comfort of their recliners? At a time when only a few networks existed in each market, small schools could not lower their prices enough to make showing their games a worthwhile proposition to television executives. Airtime was too scarce, too valuable to accommodate everyone. More than ever, the college football landscape was a battlefield of all against all. To the victors went the spoils—ticket sales *and* television revenue—while the losers would be stuck with empty stadiums and untelevised games.

***

Regional solutions were perfectly appropriate for some problems. Conferences overcame the difficulties posed by geography and logistics to forge regular schedules and develop rivalries that stoked fan interest. A national organization was not necessary for these tasks.

Other problems defied regional solution. Programs created the NCAA to solve just such a problem: the rulebook. Teams cannot play under different sets of rules. If Michigan demands a 100-yard field and Ohio State a 120-yard field, there cannot be a game unless one yields. Amateurism, at least by 1940, presented another such problem. At least conceptually, regional responses were possible for the amateurism issue, unlike the rulebook. Teams with different amateurism standards could still take the field together, though one might be at a disadvantage. The danger is that teams with different amateurism standards might come to distrust one another and refuse to play. It was this threat that caused the NCAA to introduce the Sanity Code and take a central role in defining the amateur code for the entire nation.

Television provided a third such problem for most teams. If schools had to find their own television contracts, only those schools at the top of the pyramid would earn anything from broadcasting rights. The remainder would be shut out of the television market entirely. Even worse, fans that once attended small school football games might now stay home and watch the major schools play football on television. Only a national solution could protect the small schools from television's effects.

Thus the NCAA—which, consisting of *all* schools, had many more Waynesburgs than Penns—set its sights on the television problem, appointing a Television Committee to study the question further in 1950. The committee, in turn, commissioned the National Opinion Research Council ("NORC") to determine whether television had hurt live attendance. NORC turned in its report in early 1951, and the results confirmed what the pessimists had feared. In areas where 30 percent of homes or more owned televisions, attendance at college football games declined by about 10 percent. On the other hand, in areas where only 5 percent of homes or fewer had televisions, attendance rose by about 10 percent. Correlation is not causation, but the implication was clear: more TVs meant fewer butts in stadium seats. "Unless brought under some control," NORC (somewhat hyperbolically) warned, television "threatens to seriously harm the nation's overall athletic and physical system."

Faced with this information, the NCAA abruptly ended its laissez-faire approach towards television. No longer would the NCAA forfeit control over television broadcasts to individual schools. Under the new rules, only one game per region could be televised each week. No team could appear on television more than twice in a season. For three of the ten weeks during the season, no college football whatsoever was televised. Most importantly, the NCAA would negotiate all television contracts. Live attendance was to be protected, whatever the cost.

Hardest hit by the NCAA's about-face was Penn, which had so successfully sold the rights to its games. Rather than meekly submitting, Penn challenged the new rule, pressing forward in negotiations with ABC to continue its arrangement into the 1951 season. The new NCAA policy was not legally binding; the organization could not take Penn to court if Penn televised its games. The NCAA might punish Penn, but then again, the NCAA was already punishing it by banning future television contracts. Why abide by a policy that cripples the strong for the benefit of Waynesburg?

But by threatening to continue under its contract with ABC, Penn infuriated the NCAA, which immediately pronounced Penn in "bad standing" with the association. Other colleges had to shun Penn like a leper if they hoped to remain in good standing themselves. There is unity in numbers, and had every institution—or at least some critical mass of them—chosen to shed the yoke of the NCAA in 1951, college football may have splintered into multiple organizations, some schools remaining in the NCAA and others charting their own course.

That revolution was not forthcoming. There are many Waynesburgs and few Penns. Most teams—even successful teams—benefitted by preventing other schools from poaching fans from their stadiums via television. Four schools refused to play their scheduled road games against Penn unless it adopted the NCAA television plan, thereby threatening Penn's season, television contract, and ticket sales all at once. No schools came to Penn's assistance.

Once it became obvious there would be no widespread abandonment of the NCAA, Penn's alternatives were dire. Penn could never preserve its television contract if it could not play other major schools—its season was already in jeopardy from the boycott. ABC was uninterested if there were no games to broadcast, and the network was only negligibly more interested in broadcasting games between Penn and whatever non-NCAA scrub teams Penn might hope to scrounge up. In order to play quality NCAA opponents, however, Penn would have to forfeit their television contract. Impaled on the horns of a dilemma, Penn abandoned its television aspirations in time to salvage the 1951 season.

The new television policy was not an NCAA money grab. The lion's share of the television money always made its way back into the coffers of the colleges. Teams would bicker amongst one another about how to split television revenue under the national contract, but the NCAA's share was never a major cause of dispute for the schools, large or small.

Still, the NCAA was the conduit through which all television money flowed, and as revenue grew through the years, so did the NCAA's take. Not coincidentally, the NCAA stepped up its enforcement of amateurism regulations during this period, cracking down on the regulations it installed through the 1950s and 1960s. Investigations cost money, and growing television contracts provided the cash-strapped organization with a new, much-needed source of revenue. The growth of the NCAA as an enforcement organization was symbiotic with the NCAA's newfound television negotiation authority.

That development, however, should not obscure the 1950s television revolution's true roots. At work was not bureaucratic greed, but democracy, as the many leveled the elite few. Small colleges would now find it easier to lure football fans that might otherwise have stayed home to watch the big game. As an added bonus, the smallest colleges could band together to vote themselves a disproportionate share of the television revenue. It took twelve years, but Waynesburg finally won.

***

Once a Hobbesian war of all against all, television contract negotiations became a collective enterprise amongst the schools. Yet in solving the attendance problem, the NCAA created a new set of issues. Previously, when schools negotiated their own television deals, each team was responsible for getting as much revenue for itself as possible. They were not required to share their money with any other school, unless they voluntarily agreed to do so through conference agreements. Now that all schools negotiated their television contracts together through the NCAA, a new question arose: how should they split the proceeds from those contracts amongst themselves?

There was a spectrum of possibilities. At one end of that spectrum was equality. Every Division I team—or perhaps every NCAA member, regardless of division—could receive an equal share of the television proceeds: if Penn got $10,000, Waynesburg got $10,000. While simple and egalitarian, there was no chance— even in the 1950s, with power of small schools at its highest—that such a plan could have been approved. The largest, most successful programs would never hamstring themselves in such a way. During Penn's struggle against the NCAA, the other major football powers believed they gained sufficient benefit from NCAA membership that quelling the Quaker rebellion made financial sense. Those major powers, however, would not acquiesce in a plan that paid as much money to the dregs as to themselves. Without the membership of the largest schools, the NCAA would be unable to negotiate television contracts of any value. No network would pay much for Waynesburg football.

The other extreme possibility would have been to give the broadcast money only to those schools actually televised. Only seven games were televised in 1951, the first year of the contract. If only those teams televised received television money, fourteen teams (at most) would share in the proceeds. Although the number of televised games grew over the decades, the NCAA always kept that number well below what would have been broadcast had all teams fought for their own television deals. The smallest teams went decades without appearing on television; under this plan, those teams would get no money from the television contract. Yet those small schools forced the television issue in the first place. Just on pure numbers, the smallest schools could vote some of that television money to themselves.

Another option would be to apportion money based on each team's "worth." The easiest way to determine this worth to the viewing public would be to let the schools compete on the open market for individual television contracts, but the NCAA had of course foreclosed that possibility. Yet there are other reasonably accurate methods. For example, the teams that sell the most tickets usually also draw the highest television ratings as well. Live attendance could thus be one metric for distributing television funds. Historical success might be another. Some teams are expected to compete for conference and national championships every year. Those teams are more likely to be televised, and thus should be given more money. But football can be a surprising sport; you never know when an Indiana or an Oregon State might surprise for a year and play in the must-see game of the week. Those schools' television revenues could be adjusted depending upon the chance of such a breakout season occurring. Indiana might not get as much as Oklahoma each year, but they would still get something.

This was—broadly speaking—the NCAA's solution. The details of the revenue sharing plan changed over the decades as power shifted on the football field and in NCAA committee rooms, but the basics remained the same. Both large and small schools got some of what they sought and gave up a bit in return. Small schools earned far more money under the NCAA contract than they could have mustered had they gone to the networks, hat in hand, seeking their own contract. The small universities also protected their ticket sales, especially on those Saturdays when no college football appeared on television.

For big schools, the new NCAA arrangement insured against the slings and arrows of misfortune. Just as the Fordham Rams shrunk from powerhouse to non-entity virtually overnight, a school could never quite be certain that their dominance was sustainable—Penn would discover this over the following years. The larger schools were restricted, but not absolutely barred from television, which became an important instrument for maintaining dominance through recruiting. Because the NCAA commandeered negotiating duties, larger schools also no longer separately incurred the costs of negotiations. They may have gotten the short end of the deal, but the large schools were not left empty-handed, either.

***

There was one more benefit to the unified NCAA television contract, available to haves and have-nots alike. When supply decreases and demand stays the same, prices rise. This is the rationale behind the cartel. If every team sold their product individually, the supply of televised college football would rise and prices would fall, assuming demand remained constant. Under the NCAA television policy, the supply of televised college football shrunk, and prices for that football rose.

Cartelization is harder it sounds, however, as the leaders of any oil-producing nation could tell you. Cartel members always have an incentive to cheat on their agreement. Imagine that you and I are the only two cupcake makers in a city, each selling cupcakes for 75 cents apiece. To make more money, we create a cartel and agree in private to raise our prices to $1.50. Since the cupcakes will cost more, fewer people will buy them, but we will be better off from the higher prices we now charge.

Now, behind your back, I run a special—two cupcakes for $2.50. I've found a clever way to undercut your price. If you adhere to our agreement, you will lose sales to me, as my cupcakes are now cheaper. So you cut your prices—two cupcakes for $2.25, three cupcakes for $3.00!—and we are off to the races. Soon, we are back to 75 cents a cupcake, where we started. We would each be better off if we both kept our prices high, but I am better off if I lower my prices, no matter what you do.

There are ways around this dilemma. If the cartel can punish cheaters, members will be discouraged from undercutting one another. Getting rid of members is not always an effective punishment for cartels, since the expelled party is then free to compete at lower prices. It hardly makes any difference if I expel you from my cupcake cartel for cheating on our agreement, for example. But if belonging to the cartel is a signal of quality, customers may be unwilling to go to non-members, even if they offer lower prices. NCAA membership offered a signal of quality to fans and television networks. If the NCAA excluded Penn for violating the television agreement, Penn might be able to offer whatever amount it wished on the open market, but it would also find that no network would be willing to purchase its product at *any* price. The punishment of removal from the cartel can thus sometimes keep conspirators in line.

Expulsion is not the only solution. Returning to the cupcake example, imagine that you and I enter into a contract specifying how many cupcakes each person should bake (remember, lowering supply and raising prices is essentially the same thing, since fewer people will buy cupcakes if you raise their price). If either party cheats and bakes too many cupcakes, the other cartel member might take the cheater to court and ask a judge to enforce the contract. Even without a contract, just talking to one another about our cartel on a regular basis would probably be helpful. I could assure you, and you could assure me, that we are not taking measures to compete behind one another's back. Cartels, like marriages, thrive on communication.

There is only one problem with the "contract and communicate" solution—cartelization is illegal. The Sherman Act, passed by Congress in 1890, prohibits all contracts, combinations, and conspiracies that restrain trade. Plenty of other federal and state antitrust statutes regulate behavior in this area as well. The Supreme Court has limited the Sherman Act's scope to only "unreasonable" restraints on trade, but for over a century, courts have considered cartelization one of these unreasonable restraints. In fact, the Supreme Court has ruled that cartelization is *per se*— that is, always—unreasonable and therefore illegal. Merely discussing the possibility of fixing prices with competitors is a conspiracy to commit federal law and can be similarly punished under the Sherman Act.

The NCAA was aware of this potential legal problem in the 1950s, a time when the antitrust laws were quite in vogue. Yet there were reasons to think the centralized NCAA television contract might survive legal scrutiny. The government may bring civil or criminal antitrust charges against suspected cartel members, but government resources are limited, and the case against the NCAA was not a slam-dunk. The television contract was one of a bundle of policies the NCAA justified as being necessary for preserving the sport, including the various regulations pertaining to the amateur code. If college football were reduced to being merely a minor league for the NFL, interest in the sport would plummet. The television networks were not offering hundreds of thousands of dollars to show minor league baseball, after all. By restricting the number of games on television, the NCAA argued, college football maintained its genteel and non-commercial natures.

The NCAA could also plausibly claim that their plan was not cartelization at all, but instead a necessary measure for competing effectively with other forms of entertainment. Professional leagues manage the time and number of games that appear on television, and they do so in a way that maximizes their revenue and helps them compete against other forms of entertainment. The NCAA argued that by restricting the number of games on television, it kept college football fresh for the public, which might turn away from the sport if inundated by it.

Moreover, competitors within a sports organization may reach agreements that competitors in other industries may not. After all, teams must agree to rules of play — size of field, size of ball, and so on — in a way that cupcake bakers do not (we could not legally agree, for example, that all cupcakes had to be two inches in diameter, or that all frosting must be pink). Many of these agreements by sports competitors will be completely benign or even necessary, and sorting the helpful from the harmful is often difficult.

Given how difficult the case against the NCAA would be, it was unlikely the government would step in to prosecute unless it felt the policy was perpetrating some overwhelming harm on the American public, which it did not. Enforcement of antitrust statutes, however, is not left only to the government. Indeed, the Sherman Act gives private parties quite the carrot to litigate antitrust matters; successful plaintiffs are entitled to an award three times the amount of their damages. If a plaintiff can prove $100,000 in damages from price fixing, the defendant must pay $300,000 in damages to the plaintiff. These treble damages provisions exist because cartels are often secret, and thus hard to detect. We know that some cartels will slip through the cracks, so we come down hard on those cartels we do catch.

Yet, for this treble damages carrot to work, there must be a plaintiff who has suffered damages with motivation to bring the case. The most logical private plaintiff against the NCAA would have been the television networks, which were now paying higher prices to televise fewer games each season. The networks, however, had no incentive to challenge the new television policy. The television stations with no college football may have preferred the old policy, since they were now unable to show any games, but good luck trying to prove in court that an inability to broadcast some unknown number of games at some lower price damaged the network. Better to save the attorney's fees and just broadcast other programming to compete against college football. And the network broadcasting college football games had even less motivation to challenge the policy. An antitrust action against the NCAA might earn back some pennies from the current contract; it also meant never broadcasting another NCAA event again.

Perhaps the advertisers on the networks could have challenged the contract, since they were ultimately the ones paying the higher prices through their commercials. But proving damages would be almost impossible for advertisers, because they were one step removed from the contract they believed might be causing them harm. Besides, advertisers liked having so many eyeballs on one network at one time, since it meant that they could target their ads to an entire demographic at once. Everyone was making money, so why kill a good thing?

***

The first cracks in the NCAA cartel were not inflicted from the outside, but formed from within. For all the benefits of banding together to create the unified television plan, the almost eight-hundred schools of the NCAA had little in common except their participation in college athletics. The largest schools competed for prestigious bowl bids, filled cavernous stadiums, and attracted national television markets. Those elite programs increasingly used their football teams as advertisements for their academics; many more sixteen-year olds know the record of the football team at State U than know where State U's cultural anthropology department is ranked (or whether State U even has a cultural anthropology department at all). The Flutie Effect of increased applications from high school students after periods of athletic success was known to college administrators well before Heisman Trophy–winner Doug Flutie's miracle Hail Mary pass against Miami in 1984. Entire universities relied on their football team's television appearances for exposure, and administrators at those schools bristled at NCAA provisions limiting their television presence.

At the same time, as dependence on television was growing, an elite cadre of teams arose to dominate college football, creating yet more tension between the haves and have-nots. The competitive landscape was uncannily stable during the 1970s. Alabama won eight SEC championships that decade, for example, while Michigan or Ohio State won at least a share of every Big Ten championship. As the best teams distanced themselves from the rabble, rivals needed every advantage to keep up. For teams in those dominant conferences, football could no longer be the world of pure amateurism and boyish simplicity still espoused (though almost never adhered to) by smaller schools.

To be fair, schools had good reason to treat football as business. Football revenue subsidizes the entire athletic department at most universities. The cost of college athletics was rapidly escalating, especially as federal mandates to promote women's sports went into effect. Many schools struggled to pay for an expanded menu of women's teams. Unless funding could be pulled from elsewhere in the school—and most athletic departments at least attempt to be self-sustaining, lest they incur the wrath of professors frustrated by their own shrinking budgets—football would have to be treated as business for non-revenue sports to survive.

In the late 1970s, a group of about sixty large programs—the entire membership of the SEC, Southwest Conference ("SWC"), Atlantic Coast Conference ("ACC"), Western Athletic Conference ("WAC"), and Big Eight, plus a handful of independent schools—established the College Football Association ("CFA"). Initially, the CFA was merely a lobbying group within the NCAA, a collection of schools hoping for a larger slice of the television revenue and more liberal regulations on how often teams could be broadcast. Penn stood alone in 1951 when it challenged the new television regulations; the CFA sought to avoid that untenable negotiating position. The CFA schools were still outnumbered within the

NCAA, but no longer could dissidents be isolated and picked off one by one.

The CFA's internal lobbying efforts were not entirely fruitless. For example, the NCAA did ease television appearance limitations during the late 1970s (although less than CFA members had hoped or asked): the 1977 television contract allowed each team up to five national broadcasts every two years, and the 1981 contract allowed six appearances every two years. The CFA also pushed for universal academic eligibility standards. That movement culminated in the 1985 passage of Proposition 48, which required incoming freshman to have earned a 2.0 GPA in core high school courses and a 700 SAT score to play intercollegiate sports. (There is also a potential cynical undercurrent to this CFA reform effort. With fewer kids eligible to play football, a greater percentage of top athletes would play for the top football schools. Marginal football programs have always struggled more with eligibility requirements than the major programs.)

Yet the CFA still felt unfairly restricted by the television appearance limitations. If the free market wanted additional Oklahoma or Georgia games to be televised, those schools should be free to pursue that opportunity, the CFA argued. Meanwhile, the rest of the NCAA membership refused to budge on how it divided the television proceeds (the perpetual struggle to cut the pie into slices large enough to satisfy everyone). The CFA's lobbying had proven insufficient to force any seismic changes on these matters. More drastic remedies were necessary.

Unfortunately for all parties, the pie was shrinking. College football's television ratings had declined steadily throughout the 1970s. CFA members believed that the NCAA's insistence on forcing networks to show Division II and III games contributed to this slump. If networks could show the games people truly wanted to watch, the CFA argued, ratings would rebound and everyone would make more money.

Conversely, the small-school delegation pointed to the substantial increase in broadcasts since the 1950s and 1960s as evidence that the market for college football viewership had become oversaturated. According to this story, fans did not have the time to watch college football every Saturday at multiple time slots, and as the NCAA diluted its television policy over the years, fan interest in the sport became diluted as well. The positions of the two sides were self-serving, of course, but the declining ratings reinforced each group's extant worldview.

This situation by 1981 had become a crisis, as the NCAA television contract once again came up for renewal. Previous contracts had run for either one or two seasons, but the 1977 contract had lasted four years. The NCAA sought to continue this practice; longer contracts shifted some of the risk of declining ratings away from the schools and onto the networks, since the price paid to the NCAA was locked far in advance. The NCAA did plan some changes for the 1981 contract, such as splitting the games between multiple networks and expanding cable television opportunities for teams. This was done partly to appease the CFA, but the NCAA also realized that there was more money to be had by going to multiple networks while still limiting the total number of broadcasts.

The 1981 contract with ABC and the Columbia Broadcasting Station ("CBS") was quite lucrative, earning the NCAA $263 million over four years, a healthy figure given sagging ratings. Yet news of the contract resolution enraged the CFA. Yes, there were more opportunities to appear on television. Yes, the networks were handing over bags stuffed with cash. But the television restrictions remained, and the sides still disagreed about how to appropriately split the money. Even worse, the new contract would once again last four years, locking CFA teams into the arrangement with ABC and CBS through the 1985 season.

These appeals failed to move the rank-and-file NCAA membership. The CFA had been given more money and more television appearances than ever before, and yet those schools still threw tantrums. And even if these problems could somehow be solved, the distrust between the groups still festered.

Into this chasm stepped the National Broadcasting Channel ("NBC"), the only national broadcasting network with no college football programming under the new contract. NBC had also recently lost the rights to broadcast the annual NCAA men's basketball tournament, leaving NBC with no college sports programming whatsoever. Like a scorned lover, NBC had no interest in comity with the NCAA merely for comity's sake.

Recognizing the split between the CFA and the rest of the NCAA, NBC hoped to divide and conquer. The network offered $180 million to the CFA members for the same four years covered by the NCAA contract. This was less than the $263 million ABC and CBS had given the NCAA, but only sixty schools would split the NBC money, not eight hundred. The NBC contract would also free the CFA members from the appearance restrictions that had dogged them since the 1950s.

Freedom from the NCAA, however, would have its price. The CFA contract and the NCAA contract were incompatible—never would ABC or CBS offer hundreds of millions of dollars to the NCAA for Ivy League and Division III football without getting the major teams as well. The NCAA would undoubtedly regard defection from its contract with ABC and CBS as mortal sin, warranting expulsion of the CFA teams. Because NCAA members could not play non-members in any sport, CFA schools would be barred from other lucrative NCAA events, such as the annual "March Madness" NCAA men's basketball tournament.

The CFA would also be responsible for negotiating other regulations amongst themselves, such as academic qualifications for student athletes. This process would be sure to expose differences amongst the CFA membership, which until this point could concentrate solely on television and their differences with the NCAA. An independent CFA would be responsible for all the functions that the NCAA currently undertook, and—unlike the NCAA—the CFA lacked the 75 years of tradition and camaraderie to fall back upon.

Making matters more complicated still, not every major football school was a CFA member. The Big Ten and Pacific-10 Conference ("Pac-10") rejected advances from the CFA, and representatives from both conferences professed their loyalty to the NCAA throughout the ordeal. If the CFA schools seceded, college football would be—at least temporarily, and perhaps permanently—cleft into two leagues, neither of which had any geographical or historic bond beyond their fondness for the 1981 NCAA television contract. Some valuable and longstanding interconference rivalries, such as the annual matchup between CFA-member Notre Dame and Big Ten-member Michigan State, could not continue.

Understandably then, many CFA members were skittish, and the group was hardly a unified bloc when it voted on the NBC television contract in August 1981. Only 33 of the 61 CFA schools voted in favor—a majority of the group, but just barely. Twenty schools voted no, five voted "present," and three schools walked out before the vote was called. Even with the majority's approval, the CFA occupied a precarious position. Each CFA school needed to sign the television contract before it could participate in the plan. The issue threatened to cleave the major conferences; four out of nine Southwest Conference schools voted against the contract, and neither the SEC nor the ACC were unanimously in favor. If any of those dissenting schools remained with the NCAA, the CFA would have to rework the conferences, destroying valuable rivalries in the process.

Greater participation was needed for one other reason: NBC could walk away from the contract if too many teams abandoned the deal, with "too many" left to the discretion of NBC. One high-ranking CFA official indicated that the plan would be infeasible unless the CFA brought at least 70 percent of its members onboard. If that figure were true, fifteen teams that did not vote for the contract would ultimately have to accept it. Maybe the CFA could persuade the "present" voters to switch, but convincing the "no" voters—never mind those that walked out completely—would be difficult.

Differences in power had generated friction between the CFA members and the rest of the NCAA. Less powerful schools within the CFA worried that the secession process might repeat itself once the CFA struck out on its own. Joe Kearney, commissioner of the traditionally weaker Western Athletic Conference, did not hold back after the vote. "This was a sad day for college athletics. It was a practice in greed and power grabbing. Are we educational institutions or football factories? And nobody is kidding us in the WAC. We're the nine teams that are the numbers 53 through 61 on the CFA totem pole and when the next cut to an even more elite group of powerful football teams comes, we will be the first lopped off."

That last part might not have been strictly true—Army and Navy were CFA members—but the point was well taken by the less powerful CFA schools. There was nothing magical about the number 61, and if the old conferences were about to be shredded anyway, who would be looking after, say, Rice or Vanderbilt next time the executioner arrived? Wouldn't a group of the top forty, or twenty, or twelve schools bring in even more money for the top schools, since they could split revenue fewer ways?

Just as the issue appeared to be reaching its fatal resolution, CFA leadership turned in a cunning display of passive-aggressiveness. The large football schools agreed to return and "accept" the terms of the NCAA television contract. Yet simultaneously, the CFA schools—led by the University of Oklahoma and the University of Georgia—sued the NCAA in federal court for price fixing and monopolization. Three decades after the NCAA asserted its power over television policy, a plaintiff had finally challenged the NCAA cartel—and that plaintiff came from within the NCAA itself.

***

Since the University of Oklahoma was the official lead plaintiff in the antitrust case against the NCAA, Oklahoma was the logical place to bring the lawsuit. The choice of venue, however, created immediate problems. The case was first assigned to Judge Luther Eubanks, a fully capable adjudicator nearing the end of his career on the bench. Judge Eubanks was also a lifelong Sooners fan—he earned his undergraduate and law degree from Oklahoma in the 1940s, and is reported to have attended every Oklahoma Sooners football game during the 1970s (not every home game; *every* Sooners game, home and away, for a decade). Since team allegiance can overwhelm the impartiality of even the wisest jurist, Judge Eubanks tried to pass the case to one of his colleagues. Unfortunately, no federal judge in Western Oklahoma felt he could impartially hear a case involving Sooners football. A judge from outside the district was needed to try the matter.

Into the affair stepped Juan G. Burciaga, a New Mexico judge with a fondness for traveling to other districts to hear cases. President Carter had appointed Burciaga to the federal bench just two years before the NCAA antitrust trial, but he had already grown somewhat tired of the Enchantment State's occasionally repetitive legal scene. Temporarily relocating to other districts was an opportunity to defeat the monotony of the federal bench. Uninterested in college football, Burciaga would not be influenced by allegiance to any team or fealty to the powerful NCAA. Indeed, one Burciaga's clerks would remark years later that the entire affair was "trivial," a reminder that what judges and lawyers consider important seldom matches the general population's interests.

While liked by those that knew him personally, Judge Burciaga—even then, in his first years on the bench—had a reputation of being icy in the courtroom. One person described

Burciaga's courtroom demeanor as "bearish and, sometimes, downright rude." Even those that remember the judge fondly admitted that he did not suffer fools gladly, and that he tended to find fools regularly in his courtroom. Yet such a no-nonsense demeanor was probably helpful for this case. The subject was a matter of national attention—if the NCAA television contract with ABC and CBS was nullified, no college football would appear on television, at least for a while—and both sides would be trying to press their luck with the young judge. Add the appearance of various head coaches and athletic directors to the mix, and the trial could have turned into a circus. To Judge Burciaga's credit, an appropriate judicial atmosphere was maintained throughout.

Antitrust litigation is never simple. Mountains of economic evidence are often necessary to prove antitrust harm; seldom are documents headed "CARTEL" or "FRAUD." Plaintiffs must usually piece together the case document by document, filtering outside economic influences while highlighting any favorable correlations that can be found. Defendants meet that mountain of economic evidence with their own still-larger mountain. Major antitrust lawsuits stretch over several years, as lawyers and economists sift through the endless morass.

This case was somewhat easier than the average antitrust lawsuit, however, since both plaintiff and defendant agreed on the most important facts. The NCAA schools combined forces to create a television contract and had done so since the 1950s; the details of those contracts were public information. The NCAA grounded its defense not in the facts, but in the law itself. Even if everything the CFA claimed were true, the NCAA argued, the accusations still did not add up to an antitrust violation. The CFA schools were free to leave the NCAA at any time. If the television policy were so harmful, why not abandon the organization? In fact, if price fixing truly were occurring, then the CFA schools *benefitted*, since they were also cartel members, so crying foul now was hypocritical. Furthermore, the NCAA claimed it did not "fix" prices. Instead, it set a "minimum aggregate price" from which the networks can negotiate upwards with individual schools.

Judge Burciaga rebuffed the NCAA on each of those arguments. First, the NCAA was a voluntary association only in the way a shotgun wedding is voluntary: you are free to leave at any time, but the consequences are grim. Penn's going-to-Canossa experience in the 1950s revealed that even schools with strong economic motives could not risk expulsion. Second, the CFA may not have suffered any harm from the price-fixing—indeed, those schools probably benefitted from it—but the CFA was not seeking damages, just an injunction telling the NCAA to stop fixing prices. The CFA need not show personal harm to ask a court to stop the NCAA from violating federal law in the future.

Burciaga next explored the NCAA's minimum aggregate price concept. The NCAA television committee provided the networks with "recommendations" for how much to pay the schools in return for broadcasting their games. The networks agreed to pay a specified minimum amount for each game, but the NCAA policy also permitted schools to negotiate with ABC and CBS for more money. There was only one problem: never did any television network pay one cent more than the amount recommended by the NCAA. The colleges had no bargaining power, as the networks would have gladly found another game to televise had any school balked at the recommended price, and the schools could not take their game to another network. The schools could not even play ABC and CBS, the two permitted networks under the contract, off against once another; if a game was slated for CBS, the schools could not negotiate with ABC.

Aggravating matters further, those NCAA-recommended payouts seemed to have no basis in reality. On September 26, 1981, Oklahoma played USC. Both teams were ranked among the top five teams in the nation. Over two-hundred regional ABC networks carried the game. On the other side of the country, Citadel played Appalachian State. Four ABC regional networks carried that game. Despite the obvious differences between the two matchups, all four schools received the exact same "recommended" payout from ABC. A free market in college football games would never have resulted in Appalachian State earning as much money as USC on the same weekend and at the same timeslot.

The NCAA also wheeled out the old arguments about live attendance and the unseemliness of profit maximization in collegiate sports once again. But the NORC study was now thirty years old, and the NCAA had commissioned the study at a time when few people owned televisions. The assumptions underpinning that research could no longer be assumed true, said Judge Burciaga. As for college football being too pristine for profit to play a central role, what exactly was the NCAA doing through its joint contract, if not profit maximization?

Somewhat peculiarly, the NCAA also argued that the television contract was necessary to preserve competitive balance. If small schools such as Appalachian State get more money than expected under the contract, then Appalachian State should be more competitive than they otherwise would be. A more competitive college football was more valuable overall, because fans of more teams would remain interested throughout the season. And if more fans stay interested, the policy could be justified as competitive because it helped college football compete with other forms of entertainment. Yet the argument seemed absurd immediately after a decade in which Alabama won eight SEC championships. How many conference championships would the Crimson Tide have won *without* the NCAA television policy? If parity was a worthwhile goal, the television contract was a crude instrument for reaching that goal.

The NCAA's final argument was its most subtle, and perhaps its strongest. Although the contract may have fixed prices for college football, there was no "college football market," the NCAA claimed, only an entertainment market. Every year, billions upon billions of dollars are spent on movies, music, television, sporting events, ballets, the opera, mud wrestling, and every other form of entertainment you can imagine. If the relevant framework is the entertainment market, the NCAA policy might actually promote competition overall, since it allows college football to compete more effectively against the other forms of entertainment.

Judge Burciaga dedicated several pages of his opinion to this argument, finding once again for the CFA. College football games were limited mostly to Saturdays in the fall. As Burciaga put it, "college football simply does not compete with shows such as 'M*A*S*H,' 'Dallas' or 'Saturday Night Live,'" (or opera and mud wrestling, he might have added), so those programs should not be included in the definition of the relevant market. Plus, "NCAA football is a unique product because of its history and tradition, the color and pageantry of the event, and the interest of college alumni in the football success of their alma mater." To those loyal fans, college football was not just another commodity interchangeable with skiing or pinochle. It was a market unto itself, all of which the NCAA controlled, and consumers would accept no substitutes.

The television policy was deemed to be price fixing, a *per se* offense forbidden by the Sherman Act. Judge Burciaga enjoined the NCAA from continuing under the contract. He also left no doubts as to his certainty in the correctness in the decision. As a New York Times reporter noted, Judge Burciaga sprinkled loaded terms like "pure speculation," "flawed," "untenable," "no merit," and "frivolous" throughout the opinion. Burciaga also ended the opinion with one last harsh rebuke: "The Court does not know and need not determine whether the NCAA administration, in formulating the controls at issue, was motivated by genuine concern for NCAA members, by a lust for power, or by rank greed. What is clear is that [the] NCAA has violated the antitrust laws, and that the Court's duty is to restore competition to this monopolized industry."

Burciaga handed down his mammoth decision—over fifty pages of small font in the Federal Reporter—only days after the 1982 football season kicked off. Since the injunction prohibiting the NCAA contract went into effect immediately, and the ABC-CBS contract was now invalid, there were fears that the sport would be blacked out from television screens everywhere. Some schools, set free from the chains of the contract that previously bound them, refused to leave. When asked about its upcoming game against Nebraska—the prime national attraction of the week, perhaps the entire season—Penn State athletic director Jim Tarman said, "Penn State has not made a decision yet what it will do about next week. But I don't think anyone will do anything harmful to college football."

And Penn State *was a CFA member*. The non-CFA teams were downright apoplectic about the decision. One Big Ten athletic director blustered that "I will not listen to or accept a single open-market bid to televise one of our football games for all the money next week or for the rest of this season. I feel morally bound to the NCAA television contract, no matter what was ruled by this judge." Those schools were prepared to test the conclusion that invalidating the NCAA contract would lead to more televised college football. In the absence of a joint contract, they claimed, they would exit the television market completely.

The Tenth Circuit Court of Appeals postponed the crisis, quickly issuing a stay on the injunction pending the inevitable appeal by the NCAA to that court. The 1982 football season continued under the ABC-CBS contract as planned while the sides prepared their arguments. Yet when the case went before the Tenth Circuit in 1983, the result was much the same. The NCAA was found to have fixed prices and monopolized the college football television market, and the contract was once again found illegal.

There was one final appeal to be made. Unlike the federal circuit courts, which must hear every appeal that litigants bring, the United States Supreme Court takes only a miniscule percentage of the cases brought to them each year. It is not enough for a case to be interesting, or for a case to broadly affect ordinary people, for the Supreme Court to spend time on it. Instead, the case must present novel legal issues—preferably, legal issues about which lower courts have disagreed. The Tenth Circuit's opinion and Burciaga's opinion the year before were on the cutting edge of antitrust law. A new breed of antitrust scholars, broadly known as the Chicago School because of its most prominent members' affiliation to the University of Chicago Law School, argued that America's antitrust statutes were interpreted as prohibiting far too much beneficial economic activity. This debate extended into the Supreme Court, where changing membership replenished the fountain of ideas informing the Court's understanding of the law. Judge Burciaga made the case sound easy in his opinion, but that confidence did not reflect the genuine divisions in the legal community on these antitrust issues.

There was one additional impetus for the Court to hear *NCAA v. University of Oklahoma*. Besides sitting on the highest court in the nation, Justice Byron White also happened to be the greatest running back in University of Colorado history. Given Justice White's unique familiarity with college football, many informed observers believed his expertise—and his vote—could prove critical.

White was also responsible for hearing matters that needed immediate resolution arising from the Tenth Circuit. Once again, just as Judge Burciaga's opinion threatened to throw the 1982 football season into chaos, the Tenth Circuit opinion upholding Burciaga's decision left the NCAA with no television contract whatsoever. Without another stay on the injunction, the teams would have only a few months to arrange individual contracts, and much of the 1983 season might have gone untelevised.

The former Colorado Buffaloes running back tipped his hand when he ordered an additional stay on the injunction nullifying the NCAA contract. The Supreme Court would be unable to hear the case until after the 1983 season, so yet another year would tick away on the ABC-CBS contract, regardless of how the Supreme Court might eventually rule. Legal analysts interpreted the stay as a dark omen for the CFA's chances before the Court; why permit a contract to continue if the Court was just going to strike it down later?

***

There are no appeals beyond the Supreme Court, and the parties treated the matter with the gravity it deserved. The NCAA ditched its in-house counsel for the oral argument in favor of University of Chicago professor and former Deputy Solicitor General Frank Easterbrook—an intimidating, arrogant, and supremely talented man unaccustomed to losing on the highest stage. Easterbrook was one of the reasons the Chicago School of antitrust scholarship was *called* the Chicago School; his antitrust textbook is still widely in use. His presence alone was an impressive reminder of the strength of the NCAA's arguments.

Each side is given thirty minutes to argue before the Supreme Court. Unlike a trial, where attorneys have hours to make uninterrupted opening and closing statements, oral arguments before the Supreme Court are a Socratic experience. The lawyer begins with an opening statement, which is inevitably cut off by questions from the justices within a minute or two. That back-and-forth generally continues for remaining half-hour, with counsel maybe given one or two more chances to return to their script once the justices are satisfied that they have exhausted a line of questions.

Yet Easterbrook was given four uninterrupted minutes to present his opening argument. An unidentified justice then asked the simple question whether the NCAA and the colleges were non-profit institutions. Easterbrook answered that they were, and then continued, again uninterrupted, for another two minutes. Almost a quarter of the NCAA's argument time had gone entirely unopposed by the Supreme Court, as Frank Easterbrook calmly played antitrust professor, making pupils of the foremost jurists in the nation.

The critical question according to Easterbrook was whether the NCAA had "market power," a legal term of art meaning the ability to raise prices for an entire market. All the other issues— live attendance, cartelization behavior, the need to preserve amateurism, everything—could be reduced to an inquiry into market power. To win the market power argument, Easterbrook needed to convince the Court that college football was merely part of the larger entertainment market. If the NCAA were a part of this larger market, it could not raise its prices by reducing output. A single farmer cannot grow less corn and charge more for it, because buyers will go elsewhere for their corn. Similarly, so the argument goes, a single provider of entertainment cannot merely provide less entertainment and raise its prices, as consumers will switch from college football to pro football, or basketball, or the theater. Easterbrook pointed out that the number of college football games broadcast had increased over the years, along with the price paid for those games. Had the NCAA been a monopoly, he argued, a rise in games would have meant a decline in prices and a decline in revenue. The counselor conceded that the NCAA should lose the case if it failed to prove it lacked market power. This was a bold gambit; a quite complex case had been reduced to just one question.

If the NCAA was not a monopoly, however—that is, if the NCAA lacked market power—the television agreement could be explained as an attempt by the NCAA to compete in the cutthroat market for advertisers. In a subtle dig at Judge Burciaga, Easterbrook argued that "it's natural for a judge who's a novice in both economics and the football business to be hesitant about embracing a novel explanation for why the NCAA has done what it has done," and stressed that judges should be hesitant to find antitrust violations where more innocent explanations (such as his) may be had.

Finally, towards the end of his half hour, Easterbrook took several questions from former running back Justice White, who proposed a hypothetical of his own:

> JUSTICE WHITE: Well, [suppose there] are two supermarkets in a large city, two chains. They agree not to compete. The only thing is that neither one of them has got 5 percent of the market. I had thought that is a violation of the antitrust laws. Is that right or not? They just agree not to compete, or they have a price. They say, here's what we're going to sell the following goods at, no higher, no less. Is that a violation of the antitrust laws?

> FRANK EASTERBROOK: If all they do is agree not to compete...

> WHITE: It isn't monopolization, is it?

> EASTERBROOK: It's clearly a violation of the antitrust laws. We have never had any doubt about that. But the NCAA is doing a great deal more than just agreeing not to compete.

> WHITE: But it's doing that much, isn't it? Maybe it's doing more, but it's doing that much.

Easterbrook stood silent for several seconds, treading lightly before answering the question. Justice White was sympathetic to the NCAA's position, but he had spotted a flaw in Easterbrook's strategy making market power predominant. In order to succeed, the NCAA would have to show not only that it had no power over the entertainment market, but also that it had not conspired to keep prices high in a subset of that market. The NCAA's defense was, in essence, that it wanted to cartelize, but couldn't. Easterbrook now understood that this defense was inadequate. But the NCAA's time was up.

***

The oral arguments took place in March 1984, somewhat late into the Supreme Court's 1983–84 term. The 1984 football season was still months away, but the Court would need time to deliberate. April and May passed with no opinions issued from the case. Commentators began speculating that perhaps *no* opinion would be forthcoming; the Supreme Court occasionally (but rarely) hears cases for a second time to clarify particular issues. If the Court decided to rehear the NCAA case, there would be no resolution until after the 1984 football season.

The delay was entirely innocent. Justice John Paul Stevens, who was writing the opinion in *NCAA v. University of Oklahoma*, also happened to be writing the opinion in another case. That other case—*Chevron v. National Resources Defense Council*—is now the most cited case in the history of the Supreme Court, so it is understandable his attention might have been elsewhere.

After months of speculation, the Court issued its ruling in late June. Once again, the judiciary vindicated the CFA. Prepared to confront Easterbrook and the NCAA on their own terms, Justice Stevens spent much of his majority opinion discussing the question of market power. Stevens, however, came to a different conclusion than that proffered by the NCAA. College football was so distinctive that it constituted its own market; college football was not just another form of entertainment, and fans could not easily substitute other activities. Since the NCAA controlled practically 100 percent of the college football market, it unquestionably had power in that market. The Court disagreed with Judge Burciaga's conclusion that the NCAA's behavior was per se invalid—Justice Stevens was willing to believe that the

NCAA television policy had *some* of the public benefits purported by the NCAA—but Stevens concluded that Burciaga's analysis clearly showed that the bad outweighed the good. Arrangements like the NCAA television agreement might not always be harmful *per se*, the NCAA plan was close enough to monopolization and price fixing to be illegal. Six other justices joined Stevens's opinion. Byron White dissented, siding with the NCAA, but the former running back failed to carry the day.

Only two months remained until the start of the 1984 football season. The Supreme Court voided the NCAA television contract for good, and unlike after the previous hearings, the NCAA could not ask another court to stay the decision. Come September, the college football television arrangement would be significantly different. But *NCAA v. University of Oklahoma* did not say how that new television plan was supposed to look, nor did it settle the rift between the hardline NCAA schools and the CFA. One particular type of television arrangement was found illegal, but nothing more was settled. The schools would have two months to solve the television riddle for themselves.

The teams were now free to sell the rights to their games individually, but this was not optimal for all the reasons that the NCAA had sought to control the process in the first place. If the Supreme Court was correct, and college football was a market unto itself, the supply of games in that market would rise drastically and prices would plummet if every team entered the market at once. There would be far more losers than winners if all simultaneously competed with all. This mayhem would not hurt only Waynesburg and its ilk; most large schools would see their television revenue decline as well.

The CFA must have recognized these problems when it sued the NCAA; its central argument had been that more televised games would lead to lower prices. Why file the suit at all if the CFA schools knew victory would result in less money for everyone? One possibility is that the CFA members gained more from advertising their schools through football than they lost from lower prices. Yet that is hard to believe. More high school students *might* be attracted to a school after seeing it on television, but many schools would *certainly* be losing money if the economic argument made by the CFA were correct. A lawsuit on that basis alone would be one heck of a gamble.

There were two other potential explanations for the litigation, both of which assume some insincerity by the CFA. The more egregious of the two possibilities is that the CFA never believed that the NCAA had market power. As Easterbrook had argued, if the NCAA lacked market power, it could not raise prices by lowering output. In this scenario, the NCAA as a whole was actually losing money by restricting the number of games sold, just as my cupcake shop loses money if it voluntarily turns down business. If the NCAA were truly doing this, some other motivation—competitive balance, preservation of the game, or any of those other reasons given to Judge Burciaga—must have been driving the NCAA television policy, not profit maximization.

The other possibility—far more likely—is that the CFA truly believed that the NCAA wielded market power. It just wanted to harness some of that power for itself. You don't need 100 percent control, as the NCAA did, to have power in a market; Pepsi and Coca Cola each have significant market power, even if neither company controls the soft drink market entirely. The CFA teams argued in court that they should have the ability to negotiate television rights individually, but their plan all along was to negotiate as a group once again after litigation was through—this time, however, as a smaller, more select group. In those teams' perfect world, the CFA would capture enough market power to again raise prices artificially while keeping total membership low enough to avoid antitrust scrutiny of their own. In other words, the CFA did not bring the NCAA litigation on the principle of the thing. They just wanted a piece of the action.

But the CFA's plan—hitting that sweet spot between ruinous competition and illegal cartelization—was too clever by half. Their television contract with ABC, signed shortly after the Supreme Court's decision, included several protections to insulate the CFA against antitrust scrutiny. CFA teams could now sell their games to other networks at earlier time slots if their game was not chosen for the ABC national broadcast. ESPN bought the rights to a nighttime national broadcast in 1985. The number of games shown each Saturday exploded, which undercut claims that the CFA was attempting to limit supply as the NCAA had done.

More importantly, the CFA was no longer the only game in town. The Big Ten and Pac-10, which had never joined the CFA, signed a competing television contract of their own for 1984 on CBS. Smaller teams signed local television contracts, something the old NCAA contract would have largely precluded those teams from doing.

Despite these changes, the Association of Independent Television Stations filed an antitrust suit against the CFA on almost precisely the same grounds that the CFA had brought its original suit against the NCAA. Because of his familiarity with the original litigation, Judge Burciaga presided over this lawsuit as well. This time, however, Burciaga rejected the claim made by the television stations, instead asserting that the CFA arrangement was close to what he had envisioned when he made his original decision back in 1982. The CFA thus accomplished the first half of its mission, avoiding antitrust liability.

Unfortunately for the CFA, its legal victory was Pyrrhic. Burciaga was confident that the new arrangement did not give the CFA undue market power because the new television deal was actually quite bad for the group. The CFA earned $12 million for the 1984 season under the ABC contract, a pittance compared to the $60 million the NCAA had received annually and the $45 million per year offered by NBC to the CFA in 1981. Even without

Waynesburg siphoning off some of the revenue, most CFA schools still came out far worse under the new deal than they had under the NCAA arrangement. The Southeastern Conference, for example, enjoyed a 35 percent increase in the number of games televised in 1984—and still saw its television revenue fall from $11.2 million to $7.5 million. The average cost for a thirty-second advertisement during the national game of the week on ABC fell from $60,000 to $15,000. And because the Supreme Court invalidated the old NCAA system, a return to the previous, more lucrative regime was impossible.

The reversal in economic fortunes left CFA leaders perplexed, almost as though they did not believe their own economic analysts during the litigation. Joe Paterno, head coach of CFA-member Penn State, pleaded with ABC to open its purse strings. "If I was an ABC executive, I would think of the stockholders. But I'm a football coach … Just because they have college football where they want it, they shouldn't bleed it."

Headaches multiplied. With the CFA and Pac-10/Big Ten split between television networks, every game between the two groups turned into a television turf war. Several games already scheduled for 1984 and beyond did not anticipate these concerns. The CFA refused CBS permission to televise any of its games, even those played on the home campus of Pac-10 or Big Ten schools. This position led to additional antitrust charges being brought against the CFA. These endless legal quarrels drained athletic departments of funds at a time when broadcasting money was hard to come by.

Nor did the CFA ever really solve the problem that had split the NCAA in the first place: when schools jointly negotiate a television contract, how should the group split revenue between stronger and weaker schools? If each team competed on the open market on its own, every school would know exactly what it deserved, since that would be what it earned. Your price *is* your value. But when the teams pooled their resources, many schools felt they were not getting their fair share. This is just what Joe

Kearney had predicted when he feared for the future of the WAC within the CFA. The WAC was never expelled, as Kearney had worried, but powerful schools within the association constantly angled for better deals. The SEC was most successful at this, and every few years the internal CFA agreement was altered to give the SEC schools a larger piece of the pie. Whether the SEC schools deserved a larger share is immaterial. The constant reevaluation process opened old wounds and left the CFA as something less than a unified whole.

Finally, the CFA lacked an effective punishment mechanism for teams that cheated on the cartel. When Penn challenged the 1950 NCAA policy, the NCAA threatened expulsion. This would have left Penn unable to play any other NCAA school at any sport. Severed from the NCAA, Penn football could never exist as anything but a husk of its former self.

The CFA did not have such a punishment. Expulsion from the CFA would simply have meant that teams could no longer participate in the group television plan, which was exactly what dissenters would be seeking anyway. Unlike the NCAA, the CFA could not prevent its members from playing football against non-members (CFA teams were already playing non-CFA teams). The CFA did not have any lucrative events in other sports, such as the NCAA "March Madness" basketball tournament, from which to exclude non-members. Schools had to ante up $50,000 as a penalty for leaving the CFA (later raised to $150,000), but these were paltry amounts.

This inability to punish those schools that wanted to leave the agreement doomed the CFA. Penn State, the most popular football program in the Northeast, defected from the group when it joined the Big Ten in 1990. One year later, Notre Dame, one of the few schools with a truly national following, signed its own television contract with NBC, further draining the CFA television contract of value. The cartel become more and more dependent upon the

SEC, now by far the largest draw the CFA could offer to television networks.

Just as chicanery amongst the television networks in 1981 set in motion the end of the NCAA television plan, struggles between the networks finished off the CFA. CBS left the college football broadcasting game in the early 1990s, instead focusing its energies on NFL broadcasts. In 1995, rival upstart network Fox outbid CBS on the newest NFL contract, leaving CBS without any football programming.

Fearing that this loss would cripple the network's ability to compete on weekends, CBS reentered the college football market. Rather than offering a contract to the CFA as a whole, however, CBS made its offer directly to the SEC, offering the conference $85 million for five years. Sweeting the deal even further, CBS promised the SEC a minimum of six national broadcasts per year; competing television networks had increasingly resorted to regional broadcasts to meet their minimum broadcasting obligations to teams. Athletic directors and coaches in the SEC believed that national television exposure would increase recruiting opportunities for the conference while establishing inroads for future national television contracts. Best of all, the SEC would not have to split the CBS money with anyone else.

Once the SEC abandoned the CFA, television networks were uninterested in the leftovers as a group. The remaining CFA conferences went their separate ways, each pursuing television opportunities on their own. In a little over a decade, the college football television market transformed from a monopoly controlled by the NCAA, to competing CFA and Big-10/Pac-10 cartels, to a competitive market of conferences fighting one another for every last dollar. Just as Judge Burciaga had figured.

Texas

Two decades after earnest Midwestern reformers created the Big Ten in 1896, representatives from a handful of Texas colleges met in Dallas to discuss a similar arrangement. After a few turbulent years, Southwest Conference membership stabilized, with six Texas colleges and the University of Arkansas joining. The schools' geographical closeness masked deep cultural divides. Southern Methodist University ("SMU"), nestled in the swankiest neighborhood of Dallas, attracted the emerging upper crust of Texas social life. Texas Christian University ("TCU"), just thirty miles from SMU down the Bankhead Highway in Fort Worth, was the school for the sons of West Texas ranchers. Baylor University in Waco was for Baptists. Texas Agricultural and Mechanical University ("Texas A&M") in College Station attracted East Texas farmers. Rice University was for budding academics. The University of Arkansas was for Arkansans. And in the state capital of Austin, the University of Texas attracted students from everywhere, a hodgepodge of the various groups that made up the Lone Star State.

The quality of play across football teams in the early SWC was remarkably even. From 1927 to 1937, six of the seven SWC schools won conference championships, and the seventh, Baylor, came within a game of winning the 1933 championship. Five of the seven teams won SWC championships during the 1950s. Dynasties rose and fell, and the Texas Longhorns won more than their fair share of championships, but overall the conference was well balanced. Since fans of every team had hope for success, attendance was strong throughout the conference, and all schools enjoyed healthy revenue. The SWC was the mid-century ideal of everything a college football conference should be.

As the economics of college football changed, however, so did that parity. Rising enrollment numbers at the large state schools—Texas, Texas A&M, and Arkansas—meant more fans and larger alumni bases than the private schools. More fans meant more tickets sold. It also meant a deeper pool of boosters upon which the athletic department could call for donations, which in turn meant better facilities.

Most importantly, more fans meant higher television ratings. The NCAA did its best to keep payouts under the television contract equitable, but some schools were simply more popular and commanded more national attention. Television revenue accounted for an increasing percentage of an athletic department's income after the 1950s, and the strongest schools demanded a slice of the pie that properly reflected their contribution to the sport's popularity.

Buoyed by their financial and competitive advantages, the cream of the conference separated and rose to the top. By 1962, President Kennedy was quipping "why does Rice play Texas?" in his famous "Because it is hard" speech extolling the space program, and matters only got worse for Rice and the other smaller schools. The Longhorns began a stretch of dominance in 1968 never before seen in the SWC, winning a share of five consecutive SWC championships and going 33–2 against their conference mates in the process.

***

Texas may have had the most fans and the most attention paid to it, but partisans of the Baylor Bears, SMU Mustangs, Rice Owls, and the rest of the motley collection of SWC fauna would not watch passively as their alma maters played foils to an era of Longhorn supremacy. Their boosters' competitive release took two forms—one unambiguously positive, and the other less so.

Much of the national (and especially southern) college football world, including the SWC, was unfortunately slow to embrace desegregation; the 1970 Texas Longhorns were the last all-white national championship team. Texas or Arkansas might survive, and perhaps even flourish, while recruiting only white athletes, since those schools usually had their choice of top white players. The SMUs and TCUs of the conference, however, were forever destined for sixth place if they only recruited athletes from the same alabaster talent pool.

One of sport's more redeeming characteristics is its ruthless meritocracy. Prejudice dies hard, and the fans cheering for a black halfback on Saturday afternoon might talk casually of "niggers" during a Friday night poker game, but even outright bigots often find their hatred dissipating—at least for a few hours—when those black athletes excel on the field. Triumphs like those of the integrated USC team over all-white Alabama in 1970 did change attitudes, even for fans of highly successful programs: adapt or die, they learned. And for coaches at programs mired in misery, a bigotry that impedes success ends careers.

In fairness to the great coaches of that era who fielded segregated teams, such as Bear Bryant at Alabama and Darrell Royal at Texas, complacency was as good an explanation as racism for persistent segregation in college football. Why chase down athletes in horrible inner-city neighborhoods when blue-chip kids from the high schools you have always recruited are available? (And in fairness to Bryant and Royal in particular, neither of which has ever been credibly accused of racism, both coaches oversaw their programs' integration, though neither coach was exactly a trendsetter in this regard). Coaches also faced resistance from their fans, who would not take it on faith alone that black athletes could play major college football. As in Tuscaloosa in 1970, those fans needed to be shown that they could have segregation or success, but not both.

Nature abhors a vacuum. Blue-chip athletes would not go unrecruited forever. If Texas and Arkansas would not tap these rich new veins of African-American high school talent, other schools eventually would, and did.

One of those early entrants to the market for black high school athletes in this region was Houston University, a commuter school independent from the major conferences with a decent, but not stellar, football history. Competing against Texas for recruits is difficult under the best of circumstances for any school. For Houston, head-to-head wars against Texas for top recruits would be folly. Instead, Houston recruited black athletes overlooked by the traditional powers.

Houston's newfound recruiting strength shaped the Cougars' approach on the field. More than perhaps anywhere else in America, Texan parents of all races ensure their children are developing their skills on the gridiron as fully as possible. But the inner-city school districts responsible for an ever-increasing percentage of African-American children had more pressing needs for their scarce resources than football, and so while those schools had tremendous athletes, those athletes were often raw. This was an added barrier to recruitment for larger schools, which did not want to spend much energy training recruits, since more polished, better-trained white high school athletes were available.

Nowhere was this more evident than at the quarterback position, where precise training is most necessary (the stereotype of the white quarterback, versus the black "athlete" who happens to play quarterback, continues to this day). Rather than turning undertrained inner-city recruits into traditional pocket quarterbacks, Houston coach Bill Yeoman adopted the "veer" offense, relying on option plays and a mobile quarterback who did as much damage with his legs as his arm.

The strategy paid off as the nationally ranked Houston teams of the late 1960s and early 1970s pummeled teams that once could have assumed victory against the lowly Cougars. After a string of top-25 seasons and years of persistent hectoring, the SWC extended an invitation to Houston in 1976. Houston won the conference championship in their very first season, defeating Texas and Texas A&M during the regular season and Maryland in the Cotton Bowl. This grand debut was no fluke; SWC championships also followed for the Cougars in 1978 and 1979. Within four years, Houston—lowly, commuter school Houston— had taken three championships in one college football's most powerful conferences.

Yet, like any investment, Houston's recruiting strategy could not yield abnormal returns forever. Houston was never the only school recruiting black athletes, and eventually the bigger powers caught on. Complacency was no longer acceptable at major programs, since their old systems were no longer working. When those programs adopted the Houston approach to recruiting, Houston's advantage disappeared. Texas and Arkansas, after all, still had bigger bankrolls, larger stadiums, and a more storied history. Racism persisted, but even most racists hated losing enough to accept black players. Once the SWC had fully integrated, Houston's willingness to recruit anyone was no longer enough to set it apart.

***

The smaller schools had a counterpunch. The cheating in the SWC was almost as storied as the football, with recruiting in Texas having retained the state's Wild West attitude. Cheating was not unique to the Lone Star State, of course. Teams throughout the nation flouted the "amateur code" from the moment the concept took shape, and NCAA penalties were insufficient to stop the transgressions. Still, the SWC teams were always just a bit more brazen than their peers, as the Texas *nouveau riche* took pride in demonstrating their passion for their favorite football programs and the extent of their wealth.

No SWC school was innocent. Not Houston, where one player was given money to pay for his girlfriend's abortion. Not TCU, where maladroit boosters handed out thousands upon thousands of dollars to recruits, all while being monitored by the NCAA (things got so bad at TCU that, shortly after taking the job in 1983, head coach Jim Wacker himself reported the program's sins to the

NCAA, earning the school probation for his honesty). Nor were the big schools—Texas, Texas A&M, Arkansas—immune, though because those programs had further to fall should they get caught, they tended to be a bit less brash in their efforts.

Southern Methodist University, however, put the comparatively penny-ante sins of its rivals to shame. The Mustangs did not have a bad football program—their 1966 conference championship was the only SWC championship won by a private school between 1958 and 1974—but they had hit a plateau, finishing over .500 only once during the 1970s. Apathy followed mediocrity; SMU's home games against the other SWC private schools sometimes failed to draw even 10,000 spectators. Only against the Texas Longhorns were sellouts assured. Filing the stadium with Longhorn fans kept the Mustangs' athletic department budget afloat, but repeated thrashings at the hands of big brother drained SMU fans of whatever enthusiasm the school had struggled to muster.

Mustangs devotees fervently believed their program, the school of Doak Walker and Don Meredith, could be salvaged. If nothing else, SMU could be mediocre in a way that would create a buzz on campus, increase attendance, and help Dallas residents remember that more than high school and professional football were played within city limits. Meanwhile, school administrators believed that football success could turn SMU into a nationally renowned university, in much the same way that football transformed Notre Dame from a small private college in rural Indiana into a perceived leader in multiple academic fields.

SMU channeled some of that compulsion to win, just as Houston had, towards wooing overlooked black high school athletes. In 1966, SMU head coach Hayden Fry—later a legend at the University of Iowa—recruited Jerry LeVias, the first black football player in SWC history (Houston had not yet joined the conference). Both Fry and LeVias enjoyed success at SMU, with the 1966 Mustangs winning their first conference championship in eighteen years and finishing the season ranked tenth in the national polls. Two years later, the Mustangs defeated Oklahoma in the Bluebonnet Bowl with LeVias manning the quarterback position. But SMU stalled during the last three years of Fry's tenure, winning four conference games in a season only once. In 1973, SMU replaced Fry with Dave Smith, who fared no better in his three years as head coach.

Recruiting black athletes was not enough; too many dominant programs had recognized the idiocy—from an athletic, moral, and public relations standpoint—of limiting themselves to white players. Houston may have scaled the heights of the SWC with their veer offense, but tactical brilliance was not the only thing that had fueled the Cougar's ascent. SMU needed a coach willing to break the rules, or to at least look the other way while rules were broken around him.

That man of low scruples and high standards was Ron Meyer, the wildly successful head coach at Division II University of Nevada Las Vegas ("UNLV"). Coaching the Rebels of UNLV was a thankless job, as Vegas residents were often transplants from other areas and uninterested in the paltry local sports scene. Las Vegas also offered more entertainment options than just about any city in America, crowding out interest for the hometown Division II college football team.

Even with those obstacles, Meyer took the Running Rebels from 1–10 the year before his hire to 8–3 in 1973 and 12–1 in 1974. Not only was Meyer winning, but he was winning with style, wearing garish suits and bringing an outsized personality to a city notoriously difficult to out-garish and out-personality. Rumors of Meyer's shady recruiting practices at UNLV appealed perversely to SMU boosters looking for any advantage in the cutthroat world of SWC recruiting.

Meyer took over SMU in 1976, just as Houston stormed the SWC. The Mustangs of the late 1970s under Meyer were no more competitive than those teams before his arrival, finishing under

.500 in each of Meyer's first four seasons. Yet there were some signs that, after more than a decade of futility, SMU had finally begun to turn a corner. The recruiting class of 1979 was particularly stunning, as Meyer landed commitments from Craig James and Eric Dickerson, the top two high school running backs in Texas that year.

Top recruits didn't just *happen* to go to Southern Methodist, and many believed that underhanded methods must have been involved. Dickerson's jaunts in his brand-new gold Pontiac Trans-Am, purchased just prior to Signing Day, did not help quell those rumors, though that car was bought by Dickerson's grandmother—or maybe Texas A&M. (James and Dickerson steadfastly deny to this day that anything improper occurred during either their recruitment to SMU or their time enrolled there.)

The commitments of Dickerson and James to SMU produced plenty of smoke, but the brightest fires burned elsewhere. Mustangs coaches made frequent trips to Houston, stopping at recruits' homes and handing out cash along the way. When not recruiting, coaches carried thousands of dollars in spending money in case someone on the team needed the cash quickly. Besides these ad hoc handouts, dozens of enterprising players negotiated for weekly payments, with wealthy boosters footing the bill for the payroll.

SMU's coaching staff faced a Sisyphean task. If the coaches did not fully commit to the dirty task of paying players, SMU would likely never succeed. But garden-variety improprieties alone could not fuel success. The other unsuccessful programs in the SWC were cheating too, but not enough to produce a winner; push too softly and the stone does not make it up the mountain. Yet SMU's profligacy, once it passed a certain level, was sure to alert the NCAA; push too hard and the stone goes tumbling down the other side. Luckily for SMU, the penalties for noncompliance early in SMU's bender of impropriety were not severe; some probation, a stern lecture from the NCAA, maybe a few Lord's Prayers, and SMU was free to go and (hopefully) sin no more.

***

There are two competing and seemingly irreconcilable criticisms of the NCAA. The first criticism finds the NCAA to be incompetent, blind to the sleaze and corruption that simmers around them. Those who hold this view cite the scandals that so frequently bubble to the surface in college sports as their main evidence—how can the NCAA be blind to what any person with common sense could see?

This keystone kops view of the NCAA ignores that the organization's task is more difficult than that of law enforcement. When a booster hands an envelope stuffed with cash to a recruit, the episode may be a violation of the NCAA rulebook and an affront to amateurism, but no laws are broken (at least usually—Congress and many states have recently passed laws prohibiting payments from agents to college athletes). Because the NCAA is not a law enforcement agency, it cannot secure subpoenas or otherwise force testimony from reluctant participants. Unwilling criminal witnesses in state or federal court are threatened with contempt; unwilling NCAA witnesses are harshly chided by investigators during scarcely attended press conferences, and not much else.

On the other hand, not being a law enforcement agency frees the NCAA from pesky hindrances like due process. This ties into the second criticism of the NCAA, which accuses an all-powerful and capricious organization of crippling programs based on circumstantial and, sometimes, spurious evidence. The Constitution provides protections to American citizens—trial by jury, guarantees of fairness, confrontation by hostile witnesses—before the government may punish them. The NCAA, however, is not the government, and the rules applied by the NCAA are not laws. Instead, the NCAA is a voluntary association of colleges applying an internal code. Schools consent to that code—lack of protections included—when they join the NCAA. If schools want more safeguards during investigations, then they can leave the NCAA.

Because the NCAA need not provide the same protections as the government, its procedures are in some ways more intrusive than a law enforcement investigation, despite the lack of subpoena power. For example, there is no college-sports equivalent to the Fifth Amendment or Miranda warning. Athletes suspected of receiving improper benefits can refuse to cooperate with investigators, but the NCAA can punish programs based on its players' silence. Counsel need not be provided for athletes at hearings, as would be required in most criminal trials. At the time of SMU's shenanigans, the NCAA did not even record players' statements or create transcripts, instead relying on handwritten notes and the often-fallible recollection of its investigators.

Nor is there any standard by which the NCAA must prove its case. When the government tries a defendant in criminal court, the prosecutor must prove the defendant's guilt beyond a reasonable doubt to a judge or jury. Yet the NCAA—acting simultaneously as prosecutor, judge, and jury—need only convince itself that violations have occurred. As one NCAA compliance officer said after announcing sanctions against a basketball program in the early 1990s, "just because we couldn't prove [the allegations] doesn't mean they didn't do it." In a court of law, an admission that the prosecutor "couldn't prove" their case gets the defendant off the hook. In the NCAA Star Chamber, close can be good enough.

How can the NCAA have so cavalier an attitude towards innocence and guilt? Unable to extract reliable testimony, the NCAA is in a tough position. Corruption in college sports is commonplace enough to be a platitude. In this sordid atmosphere, the NCAA often catches wind of scandals, yet cannot verify the details. Investigators may know that something improper is happening on a campus, but unless the NCAA can provide real evidence—names, dates, addresses, receipts, anything—offenders maintain plausible deniability. Rather than do nothing, the NCAA often comes down hard when it has the best opportunity, even if the case is less than airtight.

NCAA "convictions" carry real consequences. The ultimate penalty, theoretically, is expulsion from the organization. If all the other major colleges remained in the NCAA, there would be no opponents left for the excluded school to play, and the sports programs of the excluded college would wither. Assuming that a successful athletic department is a boon to the university as a whole, removal from the NCAA would deprive the school of a major asset in recruiting students and promoting itself to the public. The NCAA reserves the threat of expulsion for only the rankest insubordination, such as the insolence of Penn during the 1950s. Expelling teams from the NCAA is too severe for most mistakes. Even when the Sinful Seven admitted to willfully violating the Sanity Code, the NCAA failed to take this drastic step. Expulsion could backfire for the NCAA as well; there is always the fear that the excluded college will act as pied piper for other disaffected universities anxious to escape the perceived tyranny of the NCAA.

The next most powerful punishment available to the NCAA is suspension of a team from competing for a season or two. Suspension—colorfully labeled the "death penalty" by the media—has actually been used on occasion, unlike expulsion. The NCAA handed down the first death penalties against a handful of major basketball programs during the 1950s, when a series of point-shaving scandals tarnished the sport's integrity. (For those unfamiliar with sports gambling: an underdog is often "given" points by bookies to even the money wagered on each side. For example, a bet on a weaker team getting seven points pays out if the weaker team wins, or if it loses by less than seven points. Thus a weaker team can lose the game and bettors can still win money wagering on that team.) Players on prominent teams had taken money from gamblers to keep games close, so that those gamblers could win money by betting on the other team. The players were not deliberately losing games—just keeping them close—but altering the outcome of contests was a serious enough offense that entire programs were placed on suspension.

Although milder than expulsion, the death penalty is still reserved for the most heinous offenses. Some of the schools implicated in the scandals, such as Kentucky, quickly returned to prominence after their suspension ended, but most of the punished programs were ruined. For example, the City College of New York won the NCAA basketball tournament in 1950, was implicated in the point-shaving scandal one year later, and never again approached their earlier success.

Both expulsion and the death penalty are powerful weapons—too powerful, perhaps. If jaywalking were punishable only by death, no jury would ever convict. This was one problem with the Sanity Code, which provided for no punishments apart from expulsion; given the choice between acquittal and execution, many NCAA members chose acquittal. Suspension was not the ultimate punishment, but was still so severe that the NCAA eschewed it for three decades after the basketball point-shaving scandals.

Enforcement required penalties that NCAA members would not be too squeamish to implement. The Sanity Code standoff and the devastation left by the death penalty demonstrated the need for minor punishments against mundane rule breakers. First time offenders could be put on probation, perhaps. Repeat offenders might be barred from appearing on television, or from attending bowl games, or from giving their full allotment of athletic scholarships. These are still real penalties—a team barred from postseason play will have a much more difficult time convincing high school athletes to play, for example—but these punishments do not thoroughly ruin a program like expulsion or suspension. And within a graduated system such as the one the NCAA adopted, the lingering threat of utter obliteration for persistent, ongoing violators remains in the background, a weapon of last resort against rogue programs unwilling to mend their ways.

***

Despite SMU's flouting of the rules during the Meyer years, the NCAA had difficulty pinning the school down on anything serious. The NCAA investigated around 80 allegations against SMU in 1981, but could only confirm 29 of them. Of those 29 violations, most were exceedingly trivial: coaches making extra visits to high school players, photographs taken of recruits under the scoreboard at Texas Stadium, an improper game of racquetball between a coach and a recruit, $10 in entertainment money given to a recruit during a visit to campus, and so on. The NCAA had gone looking for far worse transgressions, spurred on by rival coaches familiar with the tactics Meyer used to lure athletes to SMU, but investigators came up mostly empty-handed.

Though the provable violations were minor, the NCAA knew there was more going on than they could show. The penalty handed down by the NCAA before the 1981 season was more severe than the insignificant violations suggested. SMU was placed on probation for two years and banned from bowl games and television appearances for one year. An improper racquetball game and a loose sawbuck kept SMU from its first Cotton Bowl in fifteen years as the Mustangs went on to a conference-best 7–1 record in the SWC.

The penalty stung SMU fans, as the NCAA bowl ban kept them from seeing their Mustangs play on the biggest stage in SWC football. Teams throughout Texas were doing worse things than the NCAA had proven. Furthermore, investigators had found no reliable evidence for the more serious accusations levied against the Mustangs. Many fans believed that the NCAA punished SMU so that an example could be made of somebody. Better to put the hammer down on SMU while the NCAA protected the real cash cows in Austin and elsewhere (a variation on the claim UNLV head basketball coach Jerry Tarkanian would make years later: "The NCAA is so mad at Kentucky, it's going to give Cleveland State two more years' probation.")

Yet at least SMU had finally scaled the SWC. After over a decade of middling results, SMU broke through in 1981 with the first ten-win season in program history and a #5 ranking in the national AP poll. And better days were still ahead. The bowl ban ended after 1981, so SMU could return to the postseason with another successful year. Craig James and Eric Dickerson were entering their senior seasons. Texas was in decline following the retirement of Darrell Royal, Houston had fallen back to Earth, and the Mustangs were the favorites to win the SWC for the first time in memory. Another year on NCAA probation wasn't enough to quell the enthusiasm, and when SMU broke through in 1982 for their first Cotton Bowl win in over thirty years, Mustangs fans could be forgiven for thinking that, finally, their moment had arrived.

SMU's success, however, was erected atop a rickety foundation, built by ineligible players and constructed of secret payouts. Like any foundation sturdy enough to build upon yet flimsy enough to crumble, SMU's edifice was susceptible to shocks outside of its control. The first of those jolts was the brazen corruption occurring at college football programs across the United States. The schools hit by NCAA sanctions during the 1980s is a Who's Who of American Colleges: Florida, Georgia, Auburn, Texas, Texas A&M, TCU, Houston, Illinois, Oklahoma, the list goes on and on. The Mustangs were poster children for that corruption, and the reaction against SMU was as much an attack on an era as it was an attack on any particular program. If the NCAA needed to make an example of someone, SMU was as good a target as any.

The second jolt augmented the first. In the 1970s, the NCAA had three functions—establishing the rules on the field, governing amateurism and academic requirements, and managing the football television contract. By the 1980s, the NCAA's hold on its television contract was slipping through its grasp, and its authority as arbiter of technical football rules was no longer a source of much power; settling details such as the length of the field was important, but that task had been mostly finished decades before. That left the NCAA with only its authority to enforce eligibility requirements. NCAA executive director Walter Byers sensed that an NCAA stripped of its football broadcast rights was an NCAA denuded of much of its power. Byers used the enforcement authority of his organization to reassert the NCAA's importance in college sports. In hindsight, it seems that programs were playing faster and looser with the rules than usual during that era, but at the same time, more than ever before in its history, the NCAA was seeking dragons to slay in an effort to preserve its own relevancy. You are always bound to find more dirt when you search for it.

SMU was cruising headlong into disaster, as its first taste of gridiron success in a generation only intensified the fans' hunger for more. The indomitable Dallas real estate tycoon Sherwood Blount was foremost amongst those boosters. Blount had played football for SMU before Meyer's arrival on campus, and he hoped to contribute more to the program than he had been able during his playing days. While many businessmen funded the SMU bankroll, Blount was open about his role, hanging around the team and frequently associating with coaches. Dressed in over-traditional Texas garb—big hats, big belt buckles, big boots— Blount was a caricature of himself, precisely the picture you draw to mind when you imagine a generic shady college football booster.

Blount, like Coach Meyer, was probably incapable of toning down his bravado, and unlike Meyer, Blount's actions were technically outside the school's control. If a booster wants to disregard NCAA rules, the school can do its best to disassociate themselves from the booster, but it cannot stop him from committing the violations.

Rogue boosters were never the problem at SMU, however, since top administrators within the school were complicit in the entire affair from the beginning. Indeed, the people in charge showed just as little self-control as Blount and the frothed fan base. It was bad enough that athletic director Bob Hitch knew and condoned the slush fund financed by Blount and others, even after the NCAA had placed SMU on probation. Even worse, knowledge of the malfeasance extended as far as Board of Governors Chairman Bill Clements and university president Donald Shields, the men who oversaw the entire university and were supposed to be ultimately responsible for ending the mayhem. Instead, the administration fueled the conflagration, or at minimum closed their eyes while the fire raged.

Such systemic corruption cannot be concealed forever. The NCAA was unable to nail down SMU on any of the worst charges in 1981 when it fell back upon the minor racquetball-related violations as grounds for punishment, but evidence of wrongdoing continued to accumulate, and a new investigation began almost as soon as the old one ended. The proud boosters that underwrote SMU's dominance did the Mustangs no favors when asked to appear before the NCAA. Sherwood Blount in particular remained defiant, maintaining that his money was for him to spend as he chose, and if that included giving cash to recruits, then so be it. The NCAA failed to appreciate this brazen insouciance. Blount's attitude towards amateurism—along with his tacit admission that athletes had been bought with his money—assured that SMU would be severely disciplined.

Punishment does not always require a conviction. Defendants often go bankrupt well before the court enters a verdict. Similarly, the uncertainty generated by investigation after investigation took its toll on the SMU football program before the NCAA could give a ruling. Top recruits shunned the program for fear of going down with the wounded ship. Coaches spent more time dealing with NCAA detectives and less time preparing their players for competition. SMU's on-field fortunes reversed. The mid-1980s Mustangs were decent squads, but no one confused those teams with the Pony Express of James and Dickerson, and never again did SMU seriously challenge for a SWC championship after 1984.

***

A new investigation into the SMU football program began in 1981, just months after the bowl ban that kept the Mustangs from the Cotton Bowl was announced. This time, the NCAA finally found some fire to accompany the smoke.

The bulk of the new violations occurred during the recruitment of offensive lineman Sean Stopperich, who was given over $10,000 from the illicit slush fund during his time at SMU despite never playing a single snap. After one season with the Mustangs, Stopperich returned home to Pennsylvania. NCAA investigators followed close behind to learn whatever they could about the program (disillusioned former players make better witnesses than happy current players, as the disillusioned ones have less incentive to hold back when questioned).

Though the NCAA did not know it then, at least a dozen players were on the SMU payroll at the time. But since none of them were talking, it was the ex-Mustang Stopperich who was essential to proving the NCAA's case. Stopperich provided a thorough accounting of what occurred from the moment SMU coaches began recruiting him until the day he left the program. These were not racquetball violations; finally, NCAA investigators had a recent former player, on record, alleging that current coaches had given him cash in return for attending SMU, and further alleging that those payments continued throughout his time there.

SMU's contempt for the rules would have to be met with an appropriately strong response from the school to satisfy the NCAA. Yet the boosters were uninterested in contrition. Some refused to give comments to the NCAA, while others stood by their actions without showing a hint of remorse. Rather than begging out of further sanctions, the donors who made the slush fund possible dared the NCAA to act, believing that whatever punishment the NCAA might dish out would pale in comparison to the boon that illegal payments had provided to the program.

Perversely, the sheer brazenness of the SMU's boosters may have somewhat shielded the Mustang program. The athletic department portrayed the "Naughty Nine" boosters bankrolling the slush fund as uncontrollable rogue agents. SMU was in too deep to cast itself as a helpless damsel in the affair, but the school could at least mitigate the damage by blaming the uncontrollable boosters. SMU administrators and coaches found a convenient scapegoat in Sherwood Blount, the abrasive new face of the college football underworld.

The punishment handed down by the NCAA just days before the 1985 season—45 football scholarships lost over two years, no bowl games for the 1985 and 1986 seasons, and three more years on probation—was among the most severe penalties ever handed down by the NCAA against a football program. Still, there was a sense by many in the program that the punishment could have been worse. By selling out the boosters—who were now absolutely banned from all program activities—the program at least lived to see another day.

One more wrong move, however, could prove fatal, and the fear of the death penalty (mostly) scared SMU straight. But what of the remaining players still promised money from the slush fund? Stopperich was gone, but several others remained with the team, and cutting them off completely could ignite a rebellion. If SMU denied the remaining players their promised payments, there was no telling what they might say in anger to the NCAA. As Sherwood Blount put it to Board of Directors Chairman Bill Clements, SMU had "a payroll to meet," sarcastically adding that Clements might "consider adding a line item to the university budget."

Continuing the slush fund carried its own risks. Just after the severe punishment was handed down against SMU in 1985, the NCAA almost unanimously authorized use of the death penalty for future repeat violators; SMU was one of the few opposing votes. Given the already unprecedented penalties levied against the Mustangs, there was almost no place left for the NCAA to go but the death penalty if SMU were caught again. Yet the shrinking number of players on the payroll gave reason for solace. Happy players do not go blabbing to the NCAA, and eventually they graduate. If SMU could just stem the tide for another couple of seasons and keep its nose clean thereafter, the program might still be rehabilitated.

The plan nearly worked. The 1985 season passed without incident, although SMU's on field performance suffered from the negativity surrounding the program. Several players on the payroll graduated after the season, leaving only a handful still receiving money from the school. Yet it only took one disgruntled player to upset the uneasy stasis that SMU had reached. Linebacker David Stanley, one of the Mustangs receiving payments, grew increasingly disenchanted during his time at SMU. Stanley saw his physical and mental health deteriorate during the 1985 season. He turned to cocaine, an expensive and unfortunate means of coping with the depression he nursed while on campus.

After two years, Stanley attempted to transfer from SMU for his final two seasons of eligibility. Head coach Bobby Collins, who took over SMU after Ron Meyer departed to the NFL in 1982, supported the transfer; Stanley leaving meant one fewer landmine upon which NCAA investigators could stumble. But after finding that no other schools wanted his services, Stanley requested to return to SMU.

Collins denied the request. With Stanley gone, Collins reckoned that SMU was one step closer to innocence. Refusing Stanley's request proved remarkably shortsighted. The former

SMU linebacker was in a unique position to dish dirt on his former team. Once severed from the payments that had preserved his wavering loyalty, Stanley felt no need to conceal the details about the continuing slush fund.

Instead of first going to the NCAA, Stanley turned to the local television media to air his grievances. Testimony from a former SMU linebacker that coaches and administrators were slipping cash under the table to current players was a bombshell—a scoop that could make a journalist's career. Yet it was also a scoop that could ruin a business. Among SMU's many boosters counted several of Dallas's most prominent businessmen. Those boosters sustained the local media though advertisements for their companies. The power to sustain implicitly includes the power to destroy, and the spigot of advertising revenue that maintains the popular media could be turned off at any time. This was not an idle threat; when the Dallas Times Herald reported Sean Stopperich's allegations, the now-defunct newspaper lost millions in ad money and never fully recovered.

Yet John Sparks, a producer at Dallas's ABC affiliate television station WFAA-TV, and Dale Hansen, the station's sports director, pressed forward. Having decided to run with the story, Sparks must have been tempted to rush the scoop to broadcast. He instead took his time and expanded the investigation beyond just the testimony of a disgruntled player, speaking also with representatives from SMU, including head coach Collins and athletic director Bob Hitch.

Stanley was a cocaine junkie, and he looked the part during the interview. The juiciest evidence often comes from untrustworthy sources, as only those who were willing to get dirty are in a position to provide information. But SMU hoped that viewers— and maybe even the NCAA—would discount Stanley's claims, at least on some subconscious level. The NCAA, notwithstanding SMU's current probationary status, might even forgive some of the violations, such as paying for Stanley's drug rehabilitation. If helping a strung-out kid get help were the worst infraction alleged, the NCAA could probably be convinced to look the other way.

All of that desperate optimism died the moment the WFAA-TV report began. The network led their November 12, 1986 broadcast with the SMU saga and, for forty unrelenting minutes, Stanley's allegations—the linebacker claimed that SMU gave him $750 per month and a $25,000 signing bonus—were aired to the greater Dallas-Fort Worth area. Along with Stanley's testimony, the most memorable part of the broadcast was Hansen's confrontation with SMU recruiting coordinator Henry Lee Parker. Hansen had obtained several envelopes used by Parker to give Stanley his slush fund money. Parker first acknowledged that the envelopes were his and then, upon recognizing what exactly the envelopes actually were, claimed the handwriting was someone else's and that he had never sent any letter to Stanley. The episode made SMU look just as guilty as it was, and Parker's ham-fisted denials were contradicted by a handwriting expert who verified that the initials on the envelope came from the recruiter's hand. Even worse, the envelope was dated October 1985—months after SMU had been placed on probation for the Stopperich affair.

By the time the forty-minute segment aired, the NCAA had already begun speaking with David Stanley; secrets of that magnitude do not remain secret for long. Any hope that SMU might get off easy vanished with the television report. Yes, SMU had hoped to draw down the slush fund until the guilty players moved on, but improper payment addition is a malady the NCAA expects schools to defeat cold turkey, not bit by bit. And the NCAA was no longer SMU's only problem. The Mustangs football program became increasingly isolated from the rest of the campus, as professors decried the win-at-all-costs culture that had taken hold in athletic department.

But even after *all that*, SMU very nearly avoided the guillotine. The SMU athletic department, faculty representatives, and NCAA enforcement agents reached a tentative preliminary agreement.

The SMU football program was banned from postseason play for several years, more scholarships would be taken away, and all key members of the coaching staff and athletic department would be fired, but the SMU football team could still play their 1987 season. Yet when the agreement was proposed by the investigators to the NCAA infractions committee—the ultimate arbiters of SMU's penalty—the recommendation was rejected. SMU had violated the rules for far too long, and far too brazenly, to avoid the death penalty once again.

If the 1985 sanctions were unprecedented, the 1987 penalty was unthinkable. The NCAA canceled SMU's 1987 football schedule entirely. SMU could play its previously scheduled road games, but no home games, in 1988, leaving only a five-game schedule that year. The NCAA extended SMU's bowl ban through 1989, while probation and scholarship reductions would continue through 1990. Ordinarily, players transferring to a new team must sit out for one year, but the NCAA allowed the remaining Mustangs to transfer immediately and without penalty—an option that all but two players chose.

Amazingly in retrospect, at least one columnist at that time decried the *leniency* of the penalty. After all, the NCAA could have canceled two full seasons of play, and the corruption displayed was about as bad as could be imagined. But most recognized just how damaging that even this tempered version of the death penalty would be. The failure of the NCAA to instate the full death penalty mattered little in the end. SMU forfeited its chance to play the permitted road games in 1988 for fear that the players on the stitched-together team would be seriously injured. The 1989 Mustangs were so depleted that new head coach Forrest Gregg, the aged former SMU lineman, outweighed and stood taller than nearly every player on his team. SMU did not win a conference game until 1992; it would not enjoy a winning season until 1997; it would not win a bowl game until December 2009, more than two decades after the death penalty.

Nor would the fallout be limited to the football field. Bill Clements, the former chairman of the SMU Board of Governors, was elected governor of Texas in late 1986, shortly after the NCAA's final investigation of SMU began. Governor Clements was directly implicated by the scandal—Sherwood Blount's comments in 1985 about a "payroll to meet" had been made to him, and Clements could not plausibly deny his knowledge of the behavior—and Clements was rendered an ineffective lame duck for almost his entire term. On the other hand, SMU accomplished something that no SWC team had ever managed before. Not even the Longhorns had ever brought down a Texas governor.

***

One of the SMU fiasco's secondary casualties was the Southwest Conference. Despite the brief ascendency of Houston and SMU, the problems that had plagued the SWC during the 1960s and early 1970s never really disappeared. Several of the conference's football programs were perpetually uncompetitive because of low enrollment levels and stingy fan support. After dominating the SWC upon its entrance, Houston spent much of the 1980s languishing at the bottom of the standings, burdened by NCAA sanctions and increased competition for African-American players. Baylor won the 1980 SWC championship, and then retired once more to mediocrity. Rice and TCU never ceased being bottom-dwellers. With SMU destroyed by the death penalty, the large state universities—Texas, Texas A&M, and Arkansas—reemerged as the SWC's reigning plutocracy.

This alone was not enough to doom the SWC—after all, SWC teams won national championships in the 1960s and 1970s despite the same competitive imbalance, and other conferences have suffered rough patches and survived. But SMU was not the only team to face the wrath of the NCAA during that period. The impulses that drove SMU to cheat drove its competitors to do the same, if perhaps on a smaller scale. Almost the entire SWC found itself on probation at some point or another during the 1970s and

1980s, playing true to its reputation as the Wild West of recruiting. Elite Texas high school athletes deserted the SWC, scared away by the dagger dangling perilously above each program.

The 1991 Cotton Bowl was symbolic of the SWC's precipitous decline. The Texas Longhorns struggled—at least by their standards—throughout the 1980s, but finally broke through in 1990 with an undefeated season within the SWC and a conference championship. Their opponent in the Cotton Bowl, the University of Miami, had spent much of the previous decade competing for national championships, but "The U" suffered a slightly disappointing 9–2 season that year. For Texas, ranked #3 in the nation before the game, the Cotton Bowl was supposed to represent the culmination of the program's rebirth.

Instead, the Longhorns long-awaited return to their state's most esteemed postseason game displayed just how far Texas— and the SWC as a whole—had fallen. After two consecutive personal foul penalties, Miami's first drive began with a first-and-forty ... which the Hurricanes successfully converted. Those two infractions would be merely the first of Miami's nine personal fouls and unsportsmanlike conduct penalties during the game. Miami broke the Cotton Bowl record for penalties before *the first half* was over.

Nevertheless, despite the Hurricanes finishing the game with 202 yards in penalty yardage assessed against them—nearly double the yardage gained by Texas's offense that day—Miami won 46–3. Even playing a team that had willingly tied one arm behind its own back, Texas could not avoid humiliation. Nor was Texas's 1991 Cotton Bowl embarrassment an isolated event. After SMU's 1983 victory over Pittsburgh, only two SWC teams would win the Cotton Bowl over the next thirteen seasons. No team from the SWC won the national championship after 1970.

Even worse, the economic rationale of the SWC had disappeared. A conference closely clustered by geography once made perfect sense. Nearby rivalries stoked fans' passions, and travel costs—once a vital consideration in an era before convenient air travel and interstate highways—were kept to a minimum. But in the post-*NCAA v. University of Oklahoma* world, television contracts outweighed those, and nearly all other, considerations. Conferences were no longer entitled to one slice of the NCAA contract, but instead fought for their own contracts in the television marketplace. The state of Texas was still interested in SWC football, since that is where all of the programs except Arkansas were located, but only two significant television markets (Dallas and Houston) fell within the Lone Star State's borders. With the product on the field declining, networks worried that the average SWC game would not attract attention outside of those two markets—and depending upon the matchup, perhaps not even there.

No matter how much the schools might swear otherwise, conference marriages are never about love. The SWC was created because it made financial sense to the participants. Once that rationale disappeared, the most attractive spouses—that is, the most valuable spouses—grew wandering eyes. Rice and TCU were fine for their time, but the breadwinners were ready for new relationships with prettier partners. Fortunately for them, there was no shortage of suitors.

Seventeen men from Ann Arbor, Michigan boarded the noon train in December 1901. Their destination was Pasadena, where sixteen of those men were to play Stanford University on the first day of the new year, with the seventeenth man, head coach Fielding Yost, on the sidelines. Travel by rail was monotonous and slow at the turn of the century. The team arrived in Duluth, Minnesota about 36 hours after its departure, greeted the handful of locals who arrived to meet the squad at midnight, and after a short break set out towards the Rockies. Three days later, the men arrived in San Francisco, where they celebrated Christmas and prepared for the final leg of their journey south towards Los Angeles.

After nearly a full week of physical inactivity aboard their Pullman cars, Michigan had only a handful of days to prepare and recondition for Stanford. Nor was this the only obstacle. Stanford had made the trip from Palo Alto across California, but Michigan had traversed half the continent with little respite apart from what it could muster while rolling the rails. There would be a few fans in Pasadena supporting the Midwestern team, but the locals were sure to be mostly antagonistic, lengthening the odds of victory further still.

Yet even with those hurdles, some predicted a Michigan victory with, as one newspaper put it, "a score as high as the moon and a cardinal death list that will depopulate Palo Alto." The 1901 Michigan Wolverines were not just a good football team; they were perhaps the best team ever fielded by a university up to that point. They may *still* be the best team ever fielded by a university, at least as compared against their contemporaries. Before the game against Stanford, Michigan had outscored its ten opponents 501–0. Only twice did opposing teams cross the

Michigan thirty-yard line all season. The Wolverines defeated Buffalo—a decent team with only two losses in 1901, not a Waynesburg-style pushover—by 128 points.

The season had officially ended in November, but Coach Yost recognized the opportunity afforded by the spectacle of his Point-a-Minute Team. Football was still considered a Northeastern sport. Though the game was still young throughout the country, football was twice as old along the Atlantic as it was in the great lakes region. The top athletes, fans thought, played at Harvard or Yale, or perhaps Princeton if they could not be admitted or recruited to the "Big Two." The athletes who remained behind to play football in the Midwest were merely the leftovers. But if Yost could take his invincible team throughout the nation—Seattle one week, Pasadena the next, Boston perhaps thereafter—that illusion of eastern dominance would forever be shattered, with Michigan recognized as every bit the equal, or superior, of the New England programs.

The best-laid schemes often go awry, and this particular scheme was not even particularly well laid. The difficulty of travel in 1901, and the difficulty of finding willing opponents, thwarted Michigan's barnstorming tour before it began. A game against the University of Washington was canceled just before the team departed for the Pacific coast; getting from Seattle to Pasadena in time for the Stanford match would simply be too arduous. As for any trip to the East Coast, just returning to Ann Arbor would take a week, by which time the players would be expected back in class. One game in Southern California would have to suffice.

Michigan's appearance in the Golden State on New Year's Day had been requested by the Pasadena Tournament of Roses Association. Since 1890, this group of semi-prominent former Easterners held festivities to celebrate the new year and, more importantly, to highlight to their brethren back on the opposite coast that the Pacific was not devoid of all entertainment and spectacle. Along with the Tournament of Roses Parade, the association staged sundry unusual events: ostrich and chariot races, rodeos, and the like. Tournament officials seized upon the popularity of football and the unique accomplishments of Michigan to launch the inaugural Tournament East-West game. As an added hook, Yost would be facing a Stanford team he had left for Ann Arbor just the year before.

Fortunately for the tournament promoters, the game was more competitive than the Buffalo-Michigan rout; unfortunately, it was not much more so. Fullback Neil Snow scored five touchdowns (still a record for the game in Pasadena) and Michigan rushed for 503 yards (also a record) in a 49–0 rout of the Cardinal. Indeed, even that score was deceptive; Stanford captain Ralph Fisher surrendered with eight minutes remaining in the game, ostensibly because of darkness. Around 8,000 people attended the match—a respectable number, but not a stunning success, and not successful enough that tournament promoters felt it imperative to restage a football game the following year. The first annual Tournament East-West game was also the last for fifteen years, as West Coast schools dropped football for rugby amidst safety concerns. Tournament officials brought back the always-popular animal races in football's stead.

Yet however much fun watching an elephant race a camel may be (the elephant won), football's popularity was unrelenting. After Stanford and Cal tossed aside its rugby rivalry and the nation's colleges adopted the standardized NCAA rulebook, tournament officials brought football back in 1916, renaming the contest the Tournament of Roses Football Game. A closer match between Washington State and Brown brought a larger audience, and the experiment pitting the best teams east and west of the Mississippi River was continued the year after, and the next year as well. Almost a century later, the Rose Bowl continues on, the Granddaddy of Them All.

The Tournament of Roses Association hoped mainly to draw interest from locals in arranging the yearly game, but soon the Rose Bowl had another happy byproduct. Fans of the lucky teams chosen to play in Pasadena used the selection as an excuse to escape winter and celebrate in the Southern California sun. Attendance skyrocketed, with crowds of more than 30,000 spectators within eight years of the contest's renewal. With tourists came tourist money, and every measure was taken to accommodate as many travelers as possible. The original Tournament Park stadium proved inadequate for the demand, so a new Rose Bowl Stadium was constructed along the Arroyo Seco riverbed, with a capacity twice as large as the old Tournament Park. For decades, Rose Bowl Stadium would seat more spectators than any other American stadium. The organizers would turn no paying fans away if they could help it.

A good idea is unlikely to remain a monopoly for long, and enterprising promoters throughout the warmer states inaugurated their own bowls in the model of the infant Granddaddy. The games adopted the colorful nomenclature of their location: the Orange Bowl in Miami, Cotton Bowl in Dallas, Sun Bowl in El Paso, Sugar Bowl in New Orleans, Citrus Bowl in Orlando. Only the names changed; the rest of the model created by the Rose Bowl remained the same. Civic groups organized, powerful teams played, excited fans spent, and local businesses appreciated their newfound tourism bounty.

Bowl games were true postseasons—that is, football season had already ended. Rivals had been vanquished or not; conference championships had been won or lost. The season ended around Thanksgiving for most teams, while the bowl games were not played until late December or early January. Some teams treated the games seriously, the culmination of a successful season. Others permitted themselves to bask in the vacation. Neither approach was incorrect—the games "mattered" only to the extent that teams believed they mattered. And in any event, bowl promoters did not mind the lax attitude teams occasionally took towards competition. The mission was to make money, and that mission was accomplished.

***

Around the same time the Pasadena Tournament of Roses Association was concocting the soon-to-be Rose Bowl game, football minds of a less entrepreneurial sort were grappling with a different problem: who is the best team in the country? That the two problems grew together was unsurprising; Fielding Yost made his trek across the Rockies to stake his claim to national superiority, after all.

The best-team question was probably unanswerable. Schools played, at most, a dozen games each year. Many played fewer. With travel being slow and unreliable, almost all schools remained in their region of the country. Several teams across America finished undefeated each season. Those unblemished teams usually had no common opponents. Often, even those opponents had no common opponents; top teams could be several degrees removed from one another. How could these teams possibly be compared, especially since, in an era before television and easy travel, literally no one in the nation could have seen each of them play?

Everyone understood there could often be no precise answer, but as anyone who has debated these things at a tavern understands, the fun is in the asking and arguing. Two methods were used for ranking the teams. The first effort at ranking was quasi-mathematical, employing whatever embryonic sabermetrics could be said to have existed in the early 20th century. University of Illinois economics professor Frank Dickerson's simple mathematical system proved popular: count the number of "strong" and "weak" victories, assign a value to each, divide by the number of games, and whichever team had the highest number would win the Dickerson National Championship, whatever that was worth.

The second group eschewed math for an "I know it when I see it" approach, preferring to subjectively weigh the plusses and minuses of each team's resume and reputation when ranking the schools. As loose and unscientific as that sounds, this was the officially preferred method of the NCAA, which asked historian Parke Davis in 1933 to announce a national champion and determine the historical national champions for every year since 1869. Davis named Michigan and Princeton the national champions in 1933, but the NCAA abandoned its efforts to name an official champion after Davis died the following offseason.

The fire had been kindled, however. Filling the void left by Davis's death, sports journalists turned to the truest experts on college football, the people who could be trusted to know exactly which team deserved to be called champion. That is, the journalists took a poll of themselves. The first, and most popular, of these polls was created by the Associated Press ("AP"), which asked its football correspondents across the country to rank teams from #1 through #20 after each week's games were finished (the poll was later expanded to 25 teams). Voters could use any process whatsoever to create their rankings. Most—inevitably—went with the simple eyeball test. Several institutions followed suit with their own me-too polls, the most significant of which was compiled by the coaches of major football teams.

Since the season ended before the bowl games, the set of rankings announcing the AP National Champion came out in late November, not January. Voters saw bowls as a reward, not a duty. Teams were not punished for goofing off a bit in Pasadena or New Orleans and not preparing as fully as possible. Yet data demands interpretation, and not counting the bowl games seemed unsatisfactory when the AP "national champion" followed their season with a loss in a bowl game.

The continuing regionalism of the sport compounded the problem. Often, multiple conferences produced viable contenders for national champion. Bowl games were the first and only chance to see those top teams pitted against one another, since the rest of the season those teams were sequestered within their conferences. Even after travel no longer posed an obstacle, it was common for southern teams to remain in the south, western teams in the west, and so on, with little admixture between the groups.

No year typified the bowl-game-interpretation problem more than 1964. After finishing the season undefeated against a tough SEC, Alabama was chosen by the AP as its champion over a similarly undefeated Arkansas team. Yet Alabama lost to Texas in the Orange Bowl—a Texas team Arkansas defeated during the season in Southwest Conference play—while Arkansas won its bowl matchup against Nebraska. Was Alabama giving a full effort in its matchup? Should it matter? National championships were mythical anyway, but watching the supposed best team in the nation lose to inferior competition rendered the "champion" label hollow (which is not to say Alabama did not claim the championship, or does not continue to do so).

After the Alabama fiasco, the AP changed its voting procedures in 1965, waiting until after the bowls to award its championship. Ironically, Alabama benefitted from this decision too. The AP ranked Michigan State #1 at the end of the year, but the Spartans dropped their Rose Bowl matchup against UCLA, while #2 Arkansas lost to LSU in the Cotton Bowl. Alabama— ranked #4 on December 31—leapfrogged three teams after their Orange Bowl victory to win back-to-back championships, albeit under markedly different circumstances. The other major polls held steadfast in awarding regular-season-only national championships for a few years, but the Coaches' Poll and the United Press International poll likewise took bowl games into account within a decade.

For better or worse, bowl games now undeniably mattered, at least if a program had any desire to win a national championship. Then again, what was a national championship? The NCAA did not award these championships. The "mythical national championship" amounted to little more than the say-so of pundits and self-interested coaches. Winning any championship was an honor, of course, but it is easy to see how a trophy given out by columnists means less than a trophy won directly from competition. And given the shortness of the season and the multitude of worthy teams each year, how could any one team ever be declared the best in absence of an extended postseason?

***

Moving the final poll to after the bowl games added a valuable data point, but was not a panacea. The first problem was the polls themselves. Ranking teams is natural. It is almost surprising that more sports have not adopted the poll system used by college football. After all, nearly every two-bit writer for every newspaper and website covering every sport publishes a list of "Power Rankings" from week to week ranking the teams. Fans in the comment sections below these articles debate why one team's record is deceptive—they were lucky! They haven't faced anyone!—and less internet-savvy fans write angry letters to the editor explaining why their team should be fifth, not seventh, in these meaningless polls. Rankings get attention. By institutionalizing these rankings, college football gained a focal point for analysis and interest.

Yet the entire polling enterprise was founded atop unstable foundations. What, exactly, did it mean to be ranked first, or sixth, or twelfth? Should the rankings be predictive, so that higher ranked teams are always expected to defeat lower ranked ones? At first blush that seems correct, but if you dig deeper the idea falls apart. Lower ranked teams commonly defeat ranked teams, and often the results are not even surprising. Las Vegas regularly makes higher ranked teams underdogs for betting purposes. If we want accurate predictors, maybe we *should* outsource the weekly polls to Vegas bookmakers. The casinos after all, unlike the pundits, have skin in the game. If Vegas makes a mistake predicting which team is better, smart bettors will steal their money.

But, if you dig a bit deeper, purely predictive rankings feel unsatisfactory. If a big favorite loses a fluky game to an underdog, there usually remains a sense that, all else being equal, the underdog should be higher ranked, although we would still pick the favorite to win a rematch. We don't give the Super Bowl trophy to the team we believe would win nine games out of ten if that team nevertheless loses the actual game. At some point, prediction must give way to results.

Maybe, then, the rankings should be purely reflexive. We can look at the resumes of the teams, see who has beaten whom, and rank accordingly. But this system—equally as intuitive as the predictive method, even if at odds with it—creates problems of its own. Often, there are irresolvable circles: Team A beats Team B, Team B beats Team C, and Team C beats Team A. Which of the three should be ranked highest? Nor is this the only problem with the resume approach. Teams in major conferences usually play much more difficult schedules, but have worse overall records. Comparing those teams to squads with better records in minor conferences is not simple.

And even if we get past the difficulties with the predictive and reflexive methods, pollsters often act entirely irrationally, refusing to drop teams in the rankings unless they lose and refusing to raise teams unless they win. If #25 goes to #1's stadium and loses in triple overtime, we might think that this reflects well on #25 and poorly on #1. Chances are, however, that #1 will remain #1 and #25 will be dropped from the rankings entirely.

Because the rankings are caught between prediction and reflection, the entire operation is irreparably flawed. That is not to say that rankings should be tossed aside. Life is messy. All systems, even if internally consistent, create their own peculiarities. But the uniqueness of college football's system— journalists guessing which team is the best—casts extra doubt on the legitimacy of any team claiming the mantle of nation's best in all but the clearest cases.

The second ranking problem came from the structure of the bowls. Every so often, the extra data point helped prevent an unworthy imposter from claiming the crown, which was exactly why the Associated Press and others moved their final polls back to January. Sometimes, the change even set the stage for the greatest games the sport has ever seen, such as the 1984 Orange Bowl between #1 Nebraska and #2 Miami. Rather than being merely an exhibition, both teams and all fans across the nation understood that the winner would be the undisputed best team in the nation.

As fantastic as that game was, the pairing of #1 and #2 was a happy fortuity, not bowl policy. The early Rose Bowl selection committees were unconstrained in their choice of teams, and because the Rose Bowl was the only postseason event, those committees did not have to worry that their love would go unrequited. If chosen for the Rose Bowl, a team would attend. This changed, however, as bowl games sprung up throughout the burgeoning Sun Belt, each bowl looking for top matches of their own. There were enough good teams to go around at first, but soon the games spread like locusts, slowed only when their appetite for quality teams went unsatisfied from lack of supply.

There was not yet any formal hierarchy—postseason was postseason, and the Cotton Bowl in Dallas technically counted for just as much as the Oil Bowl in Houston (that is, both counted for nothing). Fortunately for the more-historic games, they had a decades-long head start on the fly-by-night bowls. Earlier games had more cache with fans. Attendance was higher at the earlier bowls, which meant more revenue. Programs treated attendance at those games as a greater intrinsic reward; the Rose Bowl's heritage stretched back to the 1901 Michigan squad, while the Oil Bowl counted the not-so-historic 1943 Southwestern Louisiana team as its first victor. "Rose Bowl Champion" simply felt more important than "Oil Bowl Champion."

Anxious to cement their place at the vanguard of the college football postseason, the elite games entered into agreements with the elite conferences. Those bowl games could offer their money and prestige, if only the conferences guaranteed their champions. The Big Ten and Pac-10 sent their best teams to the Rose Bowl; the SEC, to the Sugar Bowl; the SWC, to the Cotton Bowl. The conferences were assured prime postseason placement and healthy revenue payouts, the elite bowl games were assured popular teams, and the Oil Bowl went extinct.

Because the major-conference champions were contractually attached to particular bowls, pairing the top two ranked teams in the nation was often impossible. If a Pac-10 team, for example, were ranked #1, it would be unable to play the next best team in the nation, unless the #2 team happened to be its Big Ten Rose Bowl opponent.

An even bigger problem sprung when a team from entirely outside the major conference structure challenged for the right to be called nation's best. With no prominent bowl tie-ins, these teams did not have the final opportunity presented by bowl games to defeat another powerful squad.

The first such challenger was Arizona State of the Western Athletic Conference, not traditionally regarded as one of college football's elite conferences. The Sun Devils of the late 1960s and early 1970s obliterated the WAC, but because the teams they were defeating in conference play were not good, Arizona State seldom had many impressive victories at season's end. By the end of any given year, several teams from major conferences had similar records with several better wins, if only because those teams had the chance to play better teams. In fact, the Sun Devils could not procure a bowl berth at all in 1968 despite going 8–2, and the undefeated 1969 Arizona State team had to settle for the Peach Bowl. ASU defeated all but two of its 1969 opponents by double digits, including Peach Bowl opponent North Carolina, yet still finished the year only #6 in the AP poll and #8 in the Coaches' Poll. Nor was ASU's solution as simple as scheduling tougher games. Major opponents had no interest in playing—and thereby possibly losing to—a WAC team, even if Arizona State was the best team in WAC history.

Undeterred, the WAC helped establish the Fiesta Bowl in Arizona State's backyard of Tempe. Because the WAC created the bowl, it could guarantee its champion a spot in the postseason. The strategy worked exactly how the WAC had hoped — Arizona State won four of the first five Fiesta Bowls, defeating Florida State, Missouri, Pittsburgh, and Nebraska in those games — but the WAC's victory was temporary. Arizona State's success led not to more prestige for the conference, but instead to the defection of Arizona State and Arizona in 1976 to the more powerful Pacific-8 Conference ("Pac-8," now renamed the Pac-10), robbing the WAC of its biggest draw.

Into the void left by Arizona State's departure stepped Brigham Young University ("BYU"). After the Sun Devils' departure, BYU became overlords of the WAC, drawing upon a surprisingly fertile crop of Mormon athletes across the country to dominate the Rocky Mountain region. BYU boasted a perhaps more-talented roster than those Arizona State teams, starting with quarterbacks Jim McMahon and Steve Young (he the great-great-great grandson of namesake Brigham Young) during the early 1980s. BYU's success stretched over several years, lending credibility to their claim of being a dominant program despite falling outside the major conferences. But like Arizona State before them, BYU had difficulty earning invitations from top bowls.

Outsiders such as BYU need some luck to reach the summit. Chaos is the ally of the underdog, and the 1984 season provided the perfect opportunity. BYU began 1984 unranked, as usual, but after defeating #3 Pittsburgh on week one of the season, BYU leapt to #13 in the AP poll. Pittsburgh was the final ranked team BYU faced in 1984, and even that somehow makes BYU's schedule sound more difficult than it actually was; "#3" Pittsburgh lost its first four games and finished the season 3–7–1, rightfully ignored in the final polls.

Yet the die had been cast by that early, seemingly impressive victory, and pollsters refused to drop BYU despite the accumulating evidence of Pittsburgh's putridity. Once catapulted to #13, BYU was secure at the top of the polls until they lost. Meanwhile, the remaining major contenders fell one after another, and the Cougars, by process of elimination, slowly ascended the ranks. By the season's end, BYU was the #1 team in the AP and Coaches' Polls, and the only undefeated team in the nation.

Because the WAC had no prominent bowl tie-ins (the WAC's affiliation with the suddenly prominent Fiesta Bowl ended with Arizona State's departure), BYU attended the second-tier Holiday Bowl against a disappointing 6–5, unranked Michigan team. More respected opponents, such as #2 Oklahoma, refused the matchup with BYU, claiming the mid-December Holiday Bowl would interfere with the academics of players (New Year's Day games didn't, apparently). Whatever the true reason for Oklahoma and others avoiding BYU, the 1984 Holiday Bowl victory over Michigan was both conclusive and inconclusive—conclusive because few pollsters would drop BYU from the #1 ranking after a win, and inconclusive because BYU still had not defeated a quality opponent all season.

The Cougars' championship cleft the punditry. BYU gained about two-thirds the total first-place votes of AP pollsters at the end of the season—a low figure, considering that BYU was the only undefeated team in the nation. Some journalists claimed that the championship should be left vacant, as though no possible set of circumstances in the universe could align in such a way that a school like BYU could gain entrance to the club of champions. In a sign of things to come, the New York Times developed a computer program ranking the teams, taking into account margin of victory and strength of schedule along with wins and losses. BYU came in tenth.

For the rival programs in major conferences—the athletic directors, the coaches, the boosters—the 1984 season was a stolen opportunity. In their eyes, the sport did not need another major power, and they certainly did not need another conference demanding national attention. There wasn't enough national championship to go around as it was, what with so many teams competing for the crown. Now, an outsider had swiped the rarest honor in the game. Never mind that the concept of national champions was recent, that noise and static still permeated the system, that winning the Big Eight or SEC or SWC was still a spectacular accomplishment worthy of praise and sure to draw attention from recruits and television honchos and season ticket holders. Never mind that a national championship was nothing more than the praise a few dozen journalists. Now there was a new glittering prize, a new standard against which all programs would be judged, and every member of the old guard had missed an opportunity—or, to see it their way, had an opportunity stolen away.

The furor was disproportionate to the predicament. BYU was an insider's outsider, the rare small-conference team that garnered national attention even before their rise to prominence. Much like Catholicism and Notre Dame, BYU attracted a nationwide fan base of co-religionists—in their case, Mormons—including many that did not attend the university and had no ties to Provo beyond their religion. Cougar Stadium held over sixty-thousand spectators and was comparable—favorably comparable, in many instances—to other major conference stadiums. If an outsider was going to ascend the slippery slope, BYU was as tolerable as any.

BYU's championship, however, was just part of an accelerating trend. Prior to the 1980s, the college football world had been uncannily stable. Either Ohio State or Michigan played in every Rose Bowl from 1969 to 1981. USC played in eight of those thirteen Rose Bowls. Alabama won eight SEC championships during the 1970s. Beginning in 1962, Oklahoma or Nebraska won shares of every Big Eight championship for a quarter century.

Suddenly, this cozy oligarchy disintegrated. Iowa, Illinois, and Michigan State from the Big Ten, along with stalwarts Ohio State and Michigan, attended Rose Bowls in the 1980s. Arizona State played in their first Rose Bowl in 1987. Colorado broke the

Nebraska-Oklahoma axis in the Big Eight, winning three straight conference championships from 1989–91, along with a widely recognized mythical national championship in 1990.

Nor were BYU and Colorado the only surprise national champions. The major polls voted Clemson the unanimous national champion in 1981, beginning a string of surprise national championships by formerly middle-class (or worse) programs. SMU nearly cheated their way to the 1982 championship. After decades of futility and irrelevance within even their own city, Miami won three national championships during the 1980s (1983, 1987, and 1989). Penn State won the 1982 and 1986 championships. Georgia Tech shared the 1990 championship with Colorado. Besides from SMU in 1935 and Georgia Tech in 1928 (both won at a time when the mythical national championship was not particularly prestigious or important), none of these programs had ever won a national title before their breakthrough seasons.

Further aggravating the major programs *not* winning these national championships, the newly ascendant teams took uninspiring routes to their titles. We have already seen BYU's primrose path to the crown, which included zero wins over ranked teams and a victory in the middling Holiday Bowl. Clemson went 12–0 in 1981, but the Tigers played in the relatively weak ACC, and sixty-point victories against Wake Forest were not as impressive as the lopsided scoreboard suggested. Colorado's 1990 championship came after losing an early season game against a mediocre Illinois team; the Buffaloes also needed a referee's error in the infamous "Fifth Down" game against Missouri later that season to escape from Columbia with a win. That Colorado championship was split with an equally lackluster Georgia Tech team, whose best win came over #19 Nebraska in the Citrus Bowl. The SEC and Big Ten went over a decade without a title, with strong teams from those conferences knocking one another out of the chase during the regular season while teams from weaker conferences snuck through the unlocked backdoor to the mythical championship.

***

The major-conference teams blamed the anarchic bowl system for this state of affairs. Those teams enjoyed the larger payouts given by more popular bowls, but resented that BYU could sneak past an unranked Michigan team and win a national championship. The best-case scenario for major programs was a system that maintained their stranglehold on lucrative bowls and bowl revenue while limiting the viability of the backdoor Holiday Bowl national championship strategy.

Shortly after their inception, bowl games moved away from simply inviting teams to play. There was too much competition for top schools, and television networks wanted some assurance that the matchup would be a quality one. Conferences also disliked uncertainty and preferred to lock their top few teams into particular bowl games in advance, thus guaranteeing bowl payouts to the conference before the season began. The Rose Bowl matched the Big Ten and Pac-10 champions every year; the Fiesta Bowl, at least in its early days, was required to take the WAC champion, etc. Lower bowls would lock in agreements for conferences' runners-up, third-place teams, and so on.

Because conference affiliation determined matchups, logical pairings would often go unrealized. If the #1 team in the polls were from the Pac-10 and the #2 team were from the Big Ten, the Rose Bowl would be the de facto national championship game. But if the #1 team were from the Pac-10 and the #2 team were from any conference besides the Big Ten, the two highest-ranked teams would not play one another in their final game. Both 1990 and 1991—along with many other years—ended with split national championships because the consensus #1 and #2 teams did not face one another in the postseason.

These unresolved seasons were not good for anybody. Players and programs resented their inability to "prove on the field" that they were the best in the nation. Major schools worried that a failure to make the postseason more rational favored Cinderella teams. Most importantly, conferences and bowl organizers lost the millions of dollars in increased ad revenue from pairing the best two teams at the close of the year. Television networks would pay a premium if the conferences could guarantee such a match each year.

By 1992, most of the major bowls and conferences were sufficiently tired of losing this revenue to do something about it. The SEC, ACC, SWC, Big East, and Big Eight conferences — along with their bowl partners — agreed that should the #1 and #2 ranked teams at the end of the regular season come from their conferences, those teams should be paired in their bowl game regardless of prior bowl relationships. For example, if an SEC team was ranked #1 and a SWC team ranked #2, the previous system would have sent the SEC team to the Sugar Bowl and the SWC team to the Cotton Bowl. Now, under the new Bowl Coalition, one of those teams would be moved to the other's game, creating a national championship pairing.

The system was an improvement at least insofar as there were some scenarios where a championship game would not previously have taken place but now would. But the Bowl Coalition was, at best, a half-solution. The Big Ten and Pac-10 remained committed to the Rose Bowl, fearing that opting out of that game would dilute the value of the most venerable contest in college football. The Tournament of Roses Association, still running the Rose Bowl after nearly a century, was also uninterested in letting a Pac-10 or Big Ten team go should they be ranked #1 or #2, fearing the change would void its lucrative contract with ABC. Without two of the top conferences, the Bowl Coalition was fatally flawed

***

The conferences were not forced to maintain the bowl system, even though it was the only postseason that college football has ever known. Instead, they could have established a playoff like that of every other sport. Such a tournament would have met many of the same goals as the new Bowl Coalition. Teams from smaller conferences would have to defeat at least two other top teams to win the championship, so no more BYUs could fluke their way through an easy schedule. If established creatively, the games could have been played at the bowl sites, thus preserving historic matchups and the independent value of those games. A tournament would end the split national championship phenomenon as well, although every now and again a surprising champion might cast doubt on the veracity of the tournament's results.

Several politically correct answers were available to athletic directors for why there should be no extended playoff. First, a playoff meant extra wear on players' bodies, so an extended tournament would result in more injuries. But this answer proved unsatisfactory as those same athletic directors pushed to add conference championship games and to play twelve regular-season contests rather than eleven. If player safety were such a concern, why approve schedule extensions in other contexts?

The second, related answer was that college athletes were still students, and that an extended tournament would interfere with their schoolwork. Whatever truth there might be to this, schoolwork interference did not stop those same athletic directors from pushing for ever-larger postseasons in other sports, including the Division I-AA tournament and the men's basketball "March Madness" tournament.

No doubt many people sincerely held these safety and academic concerns, but these could not have been the only motivations. Other, more worldly considerations also prevented the establishment of a playoff. For one thing, the NCAA, not the conferences, ran the tournaments in every other sport and every other division of college football. Because the NCAA ran the tournaments, the NCAA negotiated the television contracts and returned the proceeds to the schools, much as it had done for all of college football before *NCAA v. University of Oklahoma*. Less than a decade after that three-year litigation struggle, athletic programs were not about to give control of the season's most valuable games back to the NCAA.

The conferences might also have run the tournament themselves, although this solution was rife with peril. If the tournament were too big, or open to champions from all conferences, too much of the postseason revenue would be handed over to the minor conferences from the perspective of the big boys. But officially enshrining the major conferences as the only teams worthy of permanent spots in the playoff opened the conferences up to antitrust concerns and complaints that the conferences were illegally attempting to shut out the minor conferences. Several times the major conferences restructured the Bowl Coalition and its reincarnations specifically to avoid antitrust concerns, each time providing more access to smaller teams. If the major conferences were to misstep legally in creating the playoff and later be forced to allow teams from everywhere, it would be forever stuck with a system that provided too much access from their point of view. Better to move slowly and take those minor headaches as they came.

Finally, the conferences now controlled the television rights to the most important regular season in sports, and that regular season was so valuable precisely because there was no playoff at the end. Each time the postseason grew, the regular season diminished by comparison, even if only slightly. Bowl games were the devil athletic directors knew, and they also knew that a single championship game structured within that bowl system would do little to harm their cash cow. After years of a down television market and competition driving contract prices down, the conferences were finally reaping the rewards from their antitrust victory over the NCAA. It was too soon to reconnoiter a new battlefield.

Chaos

In 1844, a band of Catholic missionaries set sail from Le Harve, France for New York City. The eventual destination was the backcountry settlement of Vincennes, Indiana, but first the group would spend 39 days aboard a steamboat crossing the Atlantic Ocean. Upon arrival in New York City, the missionaries rode a second steamboat up the Erie Canal to Buffalo, then changed ships again and sailed over a violently choppy Lake Erie to Toledo. A fourth boat was taken down the Maumee River forty miles inward to Napoleon, Ohio, where a switch to canoe would be necessary to continue down the increasingly narrow Maumee.

Unfortunately for the weary travelers, the riverbeds that lied ahead were dry from the unusually arid summer. Dirt trails—often no more than a pair of rivets left by the wagon wheels of pioneers come and gone—were needed for the additional three-hundred miles separating Napoleon from Vincennes. As luck would have it, the remainder of the trip was marked by steady rain, which simultaneously filled the once-dry, now abandoned creeks and made travel by dirt trail all the more hellish.

Vincennes, founded in the early eighteenth century as a French fur-trading outpost, was the oldest settlement in the young state of Indiana; once, it had served as the capital of the entire "Indiana Territory" encompassing, Illinois, Wisconsin, Indiana, and parts of Michigan. The trappers who first invaded the region brought their Catholicism with them to the American hinterland, centering a new diocese in Vincennes encompassing all of Indiana and parts of eastern Illinois. This diocese was growing increasingly concerned that local Catholic children had only two alternatives for higher education, neither appealing to the church. The students could either head east and attend a private—likely protestant—university, or they could attend one of the provincial secular agricultural colleges.

The Le Harve missionaries were charged with finding land suitable for the creation of a proper Catholic college somewhere in the diocese's sizeable holdings. The first spot the group examined fell just across the Wabash River in Illinois. Tired from their intercontinental journey, the missionaries were satisfied with the location, but diocese leaders gently persuaded the travelers that the church could better use this land in another manner. The missionaries rejected a second spot in heavily wooded Daviess County just northwest of Vincennes as too secluded despite the already heavily Catholic presence in the area. The arduous trip from Napoleon remained fresh on the minds of the missionaries, who doubted that students would be willing to make a similar trip.

Finally, the group investigated a tract rather far afield from Vincennes, near the tiny outpost of South Bend in northern Indiana. South Bend enjoyed a few advantages; namely, reasonable proximity to Chicago and Detroit, along with a location at the apex of the Michigan Road, a well-maintained thoroughfare running through the spine of Indiana. Father Edward Sorin, the leader of the missionaries, found the land adequate for his school and dubbed his new fledgling institution, in his native tongue, Notre Dame du Luc, or Our Lady of the Lake. Within two years, the Indiana legislature granted the missionaries an official charter, and Notre Dame became the second college founded within the state.

Notre Dame was at first a university in name only, being located entirely within one building and instructing its handful of students only in the scripture and the rudiments of a handful of living and dead languages. Enrollment grew slowly over the first couple of decades, and a fire jeopardized the college's future after destroying its library and most prominent building in 1879. Nevertheless, Notre Dame persevered, and within a decade after the fire, the curriculum expanded to include non-traditional subjects such as the natural sciences and law. The university grew alongside the cities of the Midwest. Chicago, which did not even exist in 1800, boasted 1.7 million citizens by 1900, more than Vienna, Tokyo, and every U.S. municipality except New York City. A healthy percentage of that population boom came from Irish and Bohemian immigrants who brought along their Catholicism, just as the French trappers had done well over a century before.

It was also during the decade after their great fire that Notre Dame students—mimicking the more prominent schools around them, which in turn were mimicking the elite schools of the Northeast—assembled their first football team. The program began inauspiciously enough, as most college football programs did, playing only seven games total in its first five years of existence. By the turn of the century, Notre Dame played more than five games every season, though some of those games came against competition as lowly as local high schools. Notre Dame's program was not all that special—every tiny school from Wabash to Oberlin to Butler to Northwestern had a traveling football team by this point—but they were at least part of the club, one of dozens of schools amidst the burgeoning scrum.

That there were now so many colleges in this area of the nation at all would have been a shock to the missionaries who set out from Le Harve to Indiana. Several nearby territories, such as Iowa and Wisconsin, were not granted statehood until after Father Sorin founded Notre Dame, and those territories had no colleges whatsoever within their borders before their transition to statehood. The full-fledged states nearby were not much better, with only a handful apiece in the 1840s. Local populations were too sparse to support higher education, and easterners had no reason to travel to the "Northwest" for likely inferior educations.

This paucity soon ended, as America—and the Midwest in particular—experienced a higher education boom in the middle decades of the 19th century, spurred on by burgeoning populations and newfound industrial wealth. Generally speaking, there were three paths to chartering a university. The first was the Notre Dame plan, where a small group of teachers (usually, though not always, religious) bought land, held a few denominational classes, and then sought acknowledgement from the local legislature. These schools took many forms. Some looked like mini-Harvards with classes in the natural sciences, mathematics, and the like. Others were no more than pseudo-seminaries with a smattering of secular instruction thrown in.

Many education reformers grew unsatisfied with this ad hoc establishment of colleges, dependent as it was on private groups taking action, usually at a significant financial loss. Because of the private college model's perceived weaknesses, many states seized the initiative themselves, chartering schools with state funds in centrally located cities within their borders. Establishing these state colleges was sometimes a struggle. Most Midwestern states lacked significant populations, and tax collection was sporadic at best, making funding of higher education a challenging enterprise. Still, what the states lacked in funds they made up in motivation, and the chartering of a flagship university was often one of the first actions taken by the inaugural state legislatures.

But colleges cannot be run on motivation alone, and states looked to the federal government for financial support in this endeavor. For years, federal education bills were stalled in Congress by Southern legislators, who felt that the national government was not constitutionally permitted to dabble in this area. After the outbreak of the Civil War, with those Southerners now conveniently absent from Capitol Hill, Congress passed the Morrill Land Grant Act of 1862.

Under the Morrill Act, in return for chartering schools specifically dedicated to agricultural instruction and military tactics, states were granted federal land—usually in far western territories such as present-day Utah or Nevada—to sell or otherwise use as they saw fit. Most state legislatures sold the land, and then used the proceeds to establish and endow these agricultural schools. Thus began the peculiar arrangement of two major public universities in many states, one the official flagship established by state funds, and another—usually, though not always, designated by the words "State" or "A&M" or "Tech"— founded with land grant money. By 1870, most of the Midwest's major universities had been established, with the process taking a bit longer in the former Confederacy and the western territories (another land grant act was passed on much the same terms in 1890 to include the once-rebelling states).

This tripartite system of establishing colleges—private religious schools, state flagship universities, and public land-grant colleges—contributed to fierce rivalries between the schools, even apart from any sporting events. The students attending state-granted colleges modeled on more prestigious eastern universities saw themselves as more refined and intellectual than the hayseeds going to Cow College State. For their part, the aggies at the A&Ms and States of the nation pointed out that their education—going as it did towards feeding the country, protecting the homeland, and running a business—was a darn sight more practical than Ancient Greek. And both sides scoffed at the highfalutin money types attending pretend seminaries. These class rivalries anteceded football, but they found a new (*arguably* healthier) outlet once the game was introduced to campus.

***

Football was young everywhere west of the Appalachians, but it was least young in Ann Arbor, Michigan. A dozen years after the first football game between Rutgers and Princeton in 1869, modified-rugby enthusiasts at the University of Michigan accepted a gentlemen's wager from like-minded students at Racine College. The match—the first football contest west of the Alleghenies, according to a contemporaneous Chicago Tribune account—was contested at the neutral site of the Union Base-Ball Grounds in Chicago. Five hundred curious spectators watched

Michigan defeat Racine 1–0, a score that gives some indication of just how different 1879 "foot-ball" was from 1979 football.

After premature road trips through the east in 1881 in 1883 — Michigan would lose to the big three of Harvard, Yale, and Princeton within the span of a week on the first trip, and suffer three defeats in four days on the second trip — the proto-Wolverines returned to playing local colleges who, like them, were just establishing their programs. In 1887, two Michigan players suggested that the squad spread the game to Notre Dame, where those players had attended school prior to their enrollment in Ann Arbor. Michigan won an uncompetitive game against the infant program, but football took to such an extent at Notre Dame that the Catholics invited Michigan back to South Bend two more times the following spring, with Michigan winning those contests as well.

Following the games in the spring of 1888, Michigan went a decade before playing Notre Dame again. In 1896, Michigan helped found the Western Conference (now the Big Ten), a collection of the largest and most successful teams in the great lakes states. The advantages of conference membership were clear. Schedules became more consistent and easier to manage as teams played one another regularly. Rivalry between common opponents generated further interest on campuses. And, as discussed earlier, the conference framework allowed schools to address rules issues as a collective whole. The arrangement helped Michigan mature from a regional power into a national one, with Fielding Yost's dominant early 20th century teams — including the point-a-minute squad that won the first Rose Bowl — setting a new standard for football dominance.

Meanwhile, Notre Dame was building a nifty program of its own — not on par with Michigan, but a cut above the other small programs dotted across the Midwest. Notre Dame would win more games than it lost every season during the 1890s and 1900s, an accomplishment only slightly tarnished by the often watered-down competition (with everyone else doing the same thing, it seems a touch churlish to hold weak scheduling against Notre Dame alone).

By 1909, the Notre Dame program had improved sufficiently that it achieved the unthinkable. After seven previous losses, Notre Dame defeated Michigan 11–3 in Ann Arbor, scoring more points in that one game than they had in the previous matchups combined. Michigan had legitimate excuses for the loss—several key players were injured before and during the game; powerhouse Penn was on the schedule the next week, and several players likely looked past Notre Dame—and Michigan head coach Fielding Yost made sure that reporters knew all about those excuses following the match. "We went into the game caring little whether we won or lost," claimed Yost, a convenient excuse after the fact but one that carried no influence with newspapermen, who were now celebrating the pluck of Notre Dame's eleven "fighting Irishmen."

The defeat rankled in Ann Arbor to such an extent that Yost canceled Michigan's 1910 game with Notre Dame on the grounds that Notre Dame was using ineligible players. This charge was likely true, but it had been equally true in 1908, and 1902, and all those other times Michigan had thwamped Notre Dame. It was also a charge Yost could have leveled against nearly any of his opponents, or against his own team for that matter. Yost's specific complaint related to Notre Dame's high school and college being so closely intertwined. The Michigan coach believed (with some justification) that Notre Dame players were held back at the high school for additional seasoning, then released to the college team when ready for the rigors of intervarsity play. But, once again, this had been true before, yet Yost had minded these shenanigans less when Notre Dame was just another guaranteed victory on the schedule.

With the win over Michigan, Notre Dame found itself one of the largest fish in a shrinking pond. Michigan was not the only program that no longer wanted to play the Irishmen. Notre Dame struggled to schedule much beyond the chaff of the Midwest, as more established programs looked elsewhere for easy victories. A conference arrangement would have been ideal for guaranteeing major opponents, but only the Western Conference would offer the appropriate combination of difficult games and reasonable proximity for transportation. Notre Dame, along with many other schools, twice applied for membership in the conference—once at its inception in 1896, and again a decade later—but the other conference members regarded the religious school as a poor cultural fit. Leaders in South Bend believed this to be slightly concealed anti-Catholic bigotry. But Notre Dame, with its heavily religious, almost seminary-like theme, *was* a rather different beast from the other schools in the Western Conference. And while other conferences may have accepted the Irish despite their differences, Notre Dame was uninterested in accepting those offers: the other local conglomerations would have done nothing more for the Irish than mandate the scheduling of patsies.

Shut out from the conferences, voluntarily and otherwise, Notre Dame adopted a novel approach. With few opponents in the region willing and able to take on Notre Dame, the Irish wandered the country, playing major opponents wherever it could take them: Texas in Austin, Army in West Point, Princeton in New Jersey, and so on. Not all of these games ended with Notre Dame victories, but many did, and more importantly, each game provided exposure in different regions of the United States to the small Catholic school from rural upstate Indiana. The legends that grew from those years are enshrined in football lore, even today. Soon-to-be head coach Knute Rockne "invented" the forward pass as a player in a 35–13 victory against Army in 1913. Another victory over Army would inspire perhaps the most famous bit of doggerel in sports writing history, by Grantland Rice in the New York Herald Tribune:

> Outlined against a blue-gray October sky, the
> Four Horsemen rode again. In dramatic lore
> they are known as Famine, Pestilence,
> Destruction and Death. These are only aliases.

Their real names are Stuhldreher, Miller, Crowley and Layden. They formed the crest of the South Bend cyclone before which another fighting Army football team was swept over the precipice at the Polo Grounds yesterday afternoon as 55,000 spectators peered down on the bewildering panorama spread on the green plain below.

A few years later, Knute Rockne would implore his team— once again, against Army—to rally for the memory of George Gipp (the "Gipper"), a speech that would reappear in the Ronald Reagan film *Knute Rockne: All-American*.

Notre Dame skeptics can—and do—point out that none of those moments are as impressive as they are popularly remembered. The ICAA rulebook permitted the forward pass almost a decade before Rockne "invented" passing in 1913. Coaches like Chicago's Amos Alonzo Stagg and Notre Dame nemesis Fielding Yost did more to develop the pass than anyone in South Bend. The 1924 win that spawned the "Four Horsemen" moniker was a legitimately impressive upset by an Irish team headed towards an undefeated season, but the Grantland Rice passage quoted above lauding the four Notre Dame running backs is a touch overwrought for a game in which the Irish offense scored only thirteen points. And the "Gipper" speech, memorable as it remains following Ronald Reagan's adoption of it, suffers some serious continuity issues; why would a team be so inspired by the memory of a player who died *eight years before*?

But it is immaterial whether these moments deserve to be etched into the granite upon which college football's history is carved. These tales, and many others of dubious accuracy, ensnared the public consciousness during the 1910s and 1920s. By the mid-twenties, Notre Dame's place in college football was every bit as secure as, say, Michigan's—perhaps more so, because Notre Dame was building an allegiance amongst Catholics through the United States that secular public colleges could not replicate.

***

As Notre Dame ripened into a premier football program, the nearby Western Conference established itself as the leading athletic conference in the nation. National champions were not yet recognized officially or unofficially, but from 1900 to 1925, fifteen Western Conference teams enjoyed what would later be considered national championship-caliber seasons by historians. Fielding Yost's Michigan led the way, but Minnesota, Illinois, Iowa, and the University of Chicago all contributed to the tally. The balance of power in college football was shifting overland, away from the blue-blooded institutions of New England and towards the prairie.

The Western Conference was hardly a cohesive whole during its formative years. The conference's creation was principally due to its members' desire to impose academic and recruiting rules upon one another. Yet desire and execution are very different things, and some programs chaffed under their new self-imposed restrictions. Iowa was expelled from the Western Conference in 1907 after being accused of recruiting ineligible players. The conference relented four years later and readmitted the Hawkeyes, who successfully argued that they weren't doing anything worse than the other programs.

Mighty Michigan and Coach Yost also came under criticism from fellow conference members during this stretch, though the Western Conference would not dare kick out its most powerful program. They wouldn't have to: Michigan voluntarily left in 1907—the same year the Western Conference expelled Iowa—in part to escape the conference's restrictions and rules. The abandonment didn't take, as Michigan suffered several consecutive disappointing seasons soon thereafter. Before long, Michigan fans were clamoring for a return to the glory days, which included a return to the conference where those glory days occurred. The downfall was likely coincidental. Just as Harvard and Yale were losing their edge out east, Michigan could not expect to remain the only dominant program in the great lakes region forever. Still, the angst in Ann Arbor was enough to force a chastened Wolverines program back into the fold less than a decade after its departure. In Michigan's absence, and with Fielding Yost no longer around to issue a veto, Ohio State was admitted to the conference in 1912. (Without the brief spat between the Western Conference and the Wolverines, it is quite doubtful the rivalry between Michigan and Ohio State would exist as it does today, as Yost guarded the doors to the Western Conference jealously throughout his tenure in Michigan). With Michigan and Iowa returning, the conference boasted ten teams, and the colloquial name "big ten" appeared in newsprint for the first time. Soon it stuck, capitalized and official.

Conferences then were a different beast from how we know them. There was no consistent conference schedule, for example. Today, every Big Ten team plays eight conference games each season—four at home, four on the road—and the matches are set years in advance. This was not the case a century ago. In 1919, just to take one ordinary year as an example, Illinois played seven conference games, while Indiana played only two, and Purdue only three. Teams retained the power to schedule whomever they wanted, though there was a mutual expectation that programs would schedule as many fellow members as possible.

What the Big Ten did provide was an imprimatur upon member programs. An independent team's fortunes might rise and fall with the changing attitudes of recruits, but a team within a major conference had something more permanent. Iowa's expulsion and Michigan's tantrum aside, once you were inside the Big Ten, you were part of the club for good. A win over a Big Ten team meant something more, even if that something was unquantifiable. There were no polls yet, no national championships, and few postseason games. Programs existed simply to prove their superiority, and the best way of showing such proof was by defeating other top programs.

Because it was the first collection of schools to get out in front of the issue, the Big Ten had a reputation—whether deserved or not—of being less corrupt in academic and recruiting practices than other schools. Amateurism was still a very real aspiration in the 1920s, and schools that openly strayed too far from the amateur ideal endangered their popularity due to perceived shadiness. Yet despite what we might perceive as naiveté on the part of 1920s college football fans, they were no less skeptical or jaded than the fans of today. Successful college football programs faced much the same bind as baseball players at the turn of the 21st century. When everyone is assumed to be cheating, a successful program must overcome a heavy burden of proof to show that it is somehow succeeding cleanly.

The Big Ten had found the magic formula for avoiding the harshest criticism: admit only top programs, and promulgate specific recruiting restrictions (even if the rules were observed mostly in the breach). While the Big Ten dodged the worst of the firestorm over amateurism, accusations of impropriety pestered independent Notre Dame during the 1910s and 1920s as Knute Rockne's Gipper-and-horsemen-led teams were barnstorming the country. Many of these accusations, lodged by competitors, were tinged with jealousy, the sorts of allegations tossed about by the rivals of every successful program, even today.

Jealousy alone does not necessarily make accusations untrue, however, and Notre Dame did violate established norms of accepted conduct during this period in several respects. The Irish permitted freshmen teams to travel along with the varsity squad and compete against other freshmen teams, a sin in the eyes of several prominent Midwestern coaches. There were continuing concerns that Notre Dame was stashing players away in high school until they were more physically developed than the average college student; George Gipp, for example, was 25 years old during his senior season.

Insults may not break bones, but they can destroy football programs if they land squarely enough. Remember that public enthusiasm for amateurism was at an all-time high in the early 1920s, and that investigators for the Carnegie Institution were traveling the country investigating programs. Notre Dame's popularity was surging, but a string of minor scandals and innuendo could drain that popularity like death by a million mosquito bites.

Notre Dame's ongoing desire for legitimacy led Rockne to once again seek admission to the Big Ten in 1926. The Irish had applied twice before, but not since 1906; over the ensuing two decades, Notre Dame had transformed from another marginal Midwestern program into a national power. There were no doubts that the quality of the Irish program was every bit as high as that of the other Big Ten programs.

But the same fears about the appearance of impropriety that lead Notre Dame to reapply for inclusion in the Big Ten also gave conference members serious concerns. Reputation is fragile, and Notre Dame's disrepute—whether deserved or not—could have infected the conference, rather than the conference's sterling reputation—whether deserved or not—improving Notre Dame's moral standing. Trickier still, many of the accusations against the Irish had come from Big Ten coaches, who would now be deciding whether Notre Dame was pure enough for inclusion. In particular, Bob Zuppke at Illinois and, once again, Fielding Yost at Michigan led the stand against inclusion of the Irish, with both men citing fears that admission of Notre Dame would dilute the Big Ten's claim to the moral high ground.

There were also concerns about Notre Dame's otherness, for lack of a better word. Just as today with Brigham Young University, many in the Big Ten worried that Notre Dame would not be a good "cultural fit" with the other, secular schools in the conference. Catholics understandably interpreted this squeamishness unfavorably. Many claimed, and still claim today, that anti-Catholicism played a role in the Big Ten's repeated exclusion of Notre Dame from the conference. Knute Rockne in particular believed this to be true, privately referring to Fielding Yost as "a hillbilly from Tennessee [who is] very narrow on religion."

The claims of anti-Catholicism made against Yost have always been a bit flimsy, though not outlandish. The main evidence of religious bigotry proffered against Yost is, first, his refusal to play Notre Dame following Michigan's loss in 1909, and second, his public squabbling with Knute Rockne during the entirety of their careers. One hardly needs religion to explain the bickering in which the two engaged; both Yost and Rockne were stubborn men at the height of their professions, and the volleys each lobbed towards one another only deepened their mutual disrespect. The Michigan coach was also a bit of a sore loser on several occasions, so the blackballing of Notre Dame following his 1909 loss was not an exceptional event. And the Wolverines patron bristled against expansion of the conference on every occasion it was presented to him.

Unfortunately, Yost was also a man of his flawed era, refusing to play black players for example. Thus claims of prejudice against Yost are not baseless, even if the specific anti-Catholicism accusations are far from ironclad. Regardless, there was more than just prejudice at work in the exclusion of Notre Dame. Bob Zuppke of Illinois was just as adamant in his opposition to Notre Dame, yet Zuppke hired Catholics on his staff and stood by their side when bigotry within the Illinois administration endangered their positions. Similarly, Chicago's Amos Alonzo Stagg, another staunch opponent of Notre Dame's inclusion, never made a recorded statement, even privately, about the Catholic question. At best, any claim of anti-Catholicism must be intuited from Stagg's opposition to Notre Dame alone, which merely assumes the conclusion that bigotry caused his position. More likely, with the rising backlash against professionalism in college sports, many coaches were simply unwilling to spend the political capital necessary to bring a program perceived as dirty into the fray. And although its Catholicism may not have helped matters, the cause would likely have been equally doomed had Notre Dame been the State University of South Bend.

For their part, the Notre Dame administration was not completely committed to the conference experiment themselves. The school had earned its fame largely through its flexibility and willingness to play anywhere in the country. Had the Irish been tethered to the Midwestern Big Ten, these attributes may have been forever lost. Skeptics will see sour grapes—we never really wanted the Big Ten anyway, the jilted program claimed—and there might be something to that. But following their rejection in 1926 by the Big Ten, Notre Dame would stick to its story, turning down a request to join an offshoot of the Missouri Valley Conference (the eventual Big Eight) in 1928. Independence, for all its incumbent difficulties, was embraced.

***

By the 1970s, the college football conference landscape had reached stasis. The University of Chicago—founding member of the Big Ten, program of Amos Alonzo Stagg and first–Heisman Trophy winner Jay Berwanger—dropped out of the major college athletics business in 1940. A little less than a decade later, the conference, briefly the Big Nine, found a replacement in Michigan State University, accepted over the vociferous objections (as always) of representatives in Ann Arbor. That swap, Chicago for Michigan State, would be the only change to the Big Ten's membership for almost 75 years.

Out west, the Pacific Coast Conference ("PCC") consisted, circa 1930, of five natural rivalries: Washington and Washington State, Oregon and Oregon State, Cal and Stanford in Northern California, USC and UCLA in Southern California, and finally Montana and Idaho in big sky country. A slush fund scandal encompassing three of the California schools and Washington led to the disbandment of the PCC, only for the pieces to be picked up by the Pacific-8 Conference over the next few years (the big sky schools were rejected for uncompetitiveness this time around, hence the reduction from ten to eight). In 1978, the Pac-8 would swipe Arizona State and Arizona from the Western Athletic Conference, and the Pac-10 was born (more was written about this process earlier). But for as complicated as that looks, PCC/Pac-8/Pac-10 membership remained more or less stable, with the only difference between 1930 and 1980 being the trade of Idaho and Montana for the Arizona schools.

The Southwest Conference has already been discussed at length, but just to recap: after a rocky beginning that saw several schools join and quickly leave the SWC, membership finally settled by 1923 on seven programs—Texas, Texas A&M, Baylor, Rice, TCU, SMU, and Arkansas. School number eight, Texas Tech University, existed only on paper in 1923—its campus in Lubbock would come under construction a year later—but the school had grown sufficiently by the 1950s that it was a logical addition to the small, Texas-centric conference. Finally, the University of Houston would parlay an unexpected wave of on-field success into SWC membership in 1971, leaving the conference ultimately with eight Texas schools plus Arkansas. Change was slow in the SWC, with a new team added once every couple of decades following the conference's tumultuous start.

Just north of the SWC's Texas fiefdom, the schools of the Great Plains states bonded to form the Missouri Valley Intercollegiate Athletic Association, more popularly known eventually as the Big Eight. As in the SWC, membership was at first shaky, as some teams left for other conferences (Iowa to the Big Ten), others were stolen from rival conferences (Oklahoma from the SWC), and still others decided that major college athletics were not appropriate for them (Washington University in St. Louis was a founding member, for example, but went the University of Chicago route and deemphasized major athletics early in the conference's history). By the 1930's, the conference was the Big Six of Kansas, Missouri, Nebraska, Oklahoma, Kansas State, and Iowa State. In 1947, Colorado joined to create the Big Seven. Eleven years later, one-time member Oklahoma State (formerly Oklahoma A&M) would rejoin the now-Big Eight, which the conference would remain for almost four decades.

Moving back south, the final two conferences, both located largely within the former confederacy, are offspring of a common parent. While groupings like the SWC and Big Eight valued quality over quantity, the Southern Conference was a sprawling mess, encompassing 23 schools at its peak in the early 1930s. The grouping was unwieldy, too large to function as a scheduling device, and too diverse to foster agreement on major issues like scholarships and postseason play. Disputes over the propriety of athletic scholarships led thirteen Southern Conference programs to branch off and create the Southeastern Conference in 1933. Charter SEC member Sewanee made the same decision as the University of Chicago and Washington University in St. Louis, giving up the college athletics arms race in the 1940s. Tulane and Georgia Tech went independent in the 1960s, leaving the SEC with ten teams: Louisiana State, Mississippi, Mississippi State, Alabama, Auburn, Kentucky, Tennessee, Vanderbilt, Georgia, and Florida. Besides the attrition of those three schools (all of which were mostly irrelevant during their time in the conference), SEC membership remained unchanged for over a half-century.

The Southern Conference regrouped and added seven schools in 1936, only to see the secession process repeat itself when, in 1953, its eastern contingent left to form the Atlantic Coast Conference. The SEC's point of dispute with the Southern Conference had been athletic scholarships; the ACC's gripe concerned postseason play. The Southern Conference forbade members from playing in bowl games. After several years of internal wrangling, the more established football programs of the Southern Conference struck their own course. Six of the eight ACC schools—Duke, Wake Forest, North Carolina, North Carolina State, South Carolina, and Clemson—were located in the Carolinas, with Virginia and Maryland to the north rounding out the group. The ACC was, without question, the weakest of the major conferences in football during this period, winning only two national championships during the three decades following its creation (though Maryland did snag a championship in 1953, the ACC's inaugural season). South Carolina went independent in 1971, while Georgia Tech made the opposite switch in 1978, leaving the ACC once more with eight members, though now with a slightly broader geographic reach. That swap was the only change in the ACC's membership during the conference's first 35 years in existence.

The geography of the major conferences in 1977. Iowa is the only state with universities from two major conferences within its borders. From left to right and top to bottom: the Pac-10, the Big Eight, the Southwest Conference, the Big Ten, the Southeastern Conference, and the Atlantic Coast Conference. Independent schools, minor conferences, and non-football conferences are unrepresented in this map.

***

Beneath—or in some cases, alongside—the major conferences were three groups of college football programs, each an artifact of some bygone period in the sport's history.

The first group, and the most substantial in terms of on-field impact, was the independent schools. Independence is a concept unique to college sports. What would independence even mean for a professional football team? The NFL, for example, only permits its teams to play other members. A squad cannot be independent and compete within the NFL. Even if a professional league made an exception (and why would they?), an independent team by definition is ineligible to win the league championship, because they exist outside of the league. Without being able to win championships, popular interest in the team would disappear, or more likely, never appear in the first place.

Independence within the professional leagues is impossible; it is the default in college football—the state that exists in absence of a program taking the affirmative step of joining a conference. All schools were chartered—and almost all athletic departments begun—with zero consideration whatsoever paid as to which athletic conference the school would eventually join. When many universities began playing football, there were no leagues to join: no Big Ten, no SEC, and no NCAA, for that matter.

Nor were championships a sufficient carrot to compel programs to join conferences. There was no such thing as a national champion beyond the claims and arguments made by newspapermen for their preferred teams. The national championship was nothing more than reporters' opinions, and independence did not prevent teams such as Notre Dame from winning these mythical national championships, anyway.

College football's unique independence system, although peculiar, was rarely thought about much by fans while independent programs still numbered by the dozens. Independent teams had always been part of college football, dating back from the days of Rutgers and Princeton. Some great, powerful programs joined conferences, and others didn't. Some irrelevant programs remained independent, and others didn't. The state of affairs, however strange it might be, was not interesting enough to be worth contemplating.

Most of the prominent independent programs, such as Boston College, Florida State, and Miami, were located along the Atlantic coast. Many of the rest, such as Penn State and Syracuse, were relatively close by. Since football got its start in the east, many of these independent programs—especially those around New England and the Mid-Atlantic—began playing football years or even decades before conferences had been created. Their freedom from the conferences was the residue of an era in which teams simply lined up and played one another.

Independence came in two flavors. Some schools, such as Notre Dame and the service academies, remained completely removed from the collegiate conference structure. This was a tough trick to pull off. Scheduling eleven college football games every year was difficult enough, but finding new opponents each season in multiple sports—male and female, revenue and non-revenue—was a Herculean task. Because of this, some independent schools coalesced for everything *except* football, retaining freedom for the key revenue-generating sport and stability for all the rest. The most prominent of these half-a-loaf conferences were the Metro Conference, whose schools were located mostly in large Southeastern and Midwestern cities, and the Big East, whose schools were located within New England and the Mid-Atlantic region.

After independent schools, the second artifact group was the low-level programs that populated minor conferences. Beneath the ACC came other me-too conferences like the Western Athletic Conference, the most successful of the remaining bunch. The WAC was a creature of convenience for Rocky Mountain schools, which were plagued by geographic isolation from one another and from the other major-conference schools. Only with difficulty could a team like Wyoming or New Mexico convince successful programs to travel thousands of miles to their campuses. By banding together within the WAC, those schools and others like them had an easier time filling their schedules with similarly competitive teams. By the mid-1970s, the WAC boasted eight programs, including one truly strong team in Arizona State.

But the WAC's perch was a precarious one. Never did the WAC's most successful teams see membership within the conference as an ultimate goal the same way that, say, Houston felt it had "arrived" upon receiving an invitation to the SWC. So in 1978, when the Pac-8 invited Arizona and Arizona State, those schools barely hesitated before accepting the offers. The WAC was little more than a way station for upwardly mobile programs in route to their ultimate goal. A conference can only advance so far if its rivals can poach its most prominent teams at will.

Even when its strongest teams stuck around, the mere fact of WAC membership undermined the claims of those teams to national relevance. When BYU remained the only undefeated team at the end of the 1984 college football season, its weak conference schedule was used as evidence that the Cougars could not have been a true champion, that there must have been one—or several—better teams somewhere in America. As we've already seen, BYU's 1984 national championship was a weighty impetus towards a system in which an outsider had almost no chance of duplicating BYU's feat. And when the Bowl Coalition explicitly drew the insider-outsider line in 1992, the WAC fell on the bad side of the line.

Still further below the minor conferences came the third artifact group. In 1958, the NCAA cordoned off a subset of teams that were to be graded on an entirely different scale from those schools playing major college football. These divisions took a variety of names over the years, beginning with the "College Division" moniker, but the idea was always the same: an alternative was needed for schools that were unable to keep up with the rat race of top-level football. This partition also served as a handy marker for when it came time to dole out the proceeds from the NCAA television contract.

In 1973, the NCAA reworked the split into three detachments, named Divisions I, II, and III, with Division I being the highest level of play. This tripartite system proved still not finely grained enough. Many colleges with competitive basketball programs hoped to remain at Division I so that they could remain eligible for the NCAA men's basketball tournament, but lacked the money to compete on the more expensive gridiron. Three divisions also did not capture the wide variance in strength between programs, and a few Division II schools came to dominate over the rest of the pack. Finally, in 1978, Division I was split into two groups— Division I-A and Division I-AA. All four levels of play were awarded their own championships, with three of the four championships—all except Division I-A, the highest level— awarded directly by the NCAA. (The NCAA has recently renamed Division 1-A "Football Bowl Subdivision" and Division I-AA "Football Championship Subdivision." To avoid using the terms anachronistically, and for consistency's sake, I will refer to the divisions as I-A and I-AA throughout.)

Unlike the fuzzy divider between major and minor (or "mid-major") conferences, the line between the divisions was bright and clear. Schools could move up or down depending upon their competitive needs, but only Division I-A teams were eligible for the biggest prizes, regardless of whether a fluke Division I-AA or Division II team could put together a championship-level team. Such a thing was nearly impossible, anyhow. By branding oneself as belonging to a lower division, a school announced that it was no longer a serious competitor in the world of college football. Those lower programs—some fossilized, some stillborn—would continue playing football only as a curiosity for otherwise uninterested alumni, or—if taken at their most romantic—as a throwback to the days when college sports existed truly for the fitness and betterment of the ordinary college student.

***

Each major conference was its own beast, with its own peculiar history shaping its borders and attitudes, but there were several similarities amongst the groups. The first of those similarities was compactness. The drive from Ames, Iowa to Norman, Oklahoma—the most distant campuses in the Big Six—takes about 10 hours, even accounting for pit stops. The ACC's longest drive, from College Park, Maryland to Clemson, South Carolina takes under ten hours. The longest road trip within the SEC—from Baton Rouge, Louisiana to Lexington, Kentucky—clocks in around thirteen hours, while the Big Ten's Columbus to Minneapolis sojourn takes about a half-hour longer if you miss the Chicago traffic. Only in the Pac-10 were some drives unmanageable, such as the 1500+ mile trek from Tucson, Arizona to Seattle, Washington. But other than on the West Coast, committed fans could drive to any conference game they so chose, regardless of where they started their journey.

Second, every major conference stressed local rivalry. The Pac-8, and later the Pac-10, is the best example of this, with natural rivalry pairings for each institution: Washington-Washington State, Oregon-Oregon State, Cal-Stanford in Northern California, USC-UCLA in Southern California, and Arizona-Arizona State. Other conferences were not quite so tidily paired, but the same idea was present. The ten-team SEC featured two schools within the states of Tennessee, Mississippi, and Alabama, and there were also two Louisiana and Georgia teams before Tulane and Georgia Tech left the SEC in the 1960s. Half of the ACC was within North Carolina; one could wake up at 9:00 A.M. and see four ACC campuses by car before noon. In the SWC, where eight of the nine schools were in the same state, there were smaller couplings within the larger whole: Houston and Rice, TCU and SMU near Dallas, Texas and Texas A&M in the heart of the state. Conference founders and commissioners emphasized geographic overlap, both to cut down on travel costs and to increase interest amongst fans.

Finally, the teams within the major conferences had a shared history that helped define their membership. The PCC was founded as a solution to geographic isolation; the slush-fund scandals of the 1950s led the PCC schools to redefine and reassert their common amateurism goals, which in turn led to the creation of the Pac-8. The Big Ten was formed in much the same fashion, and for much the same reasons, a half-century earlier. The SEC was created in an effort to legitimate the use of athletic scholarships, while the ACC was formed in support of postseason play. These histories may not always have been in the foreground of the relationships between schools, but the strongest conferences had been forged in the crucible of crisis, and those stressful origins drove the conferences to define themselves, from the moment of their inception, as something more substantive than merely a group of schools that happened to play football against one another on a regular basis.

All three of those rationales—proximity, rivalry, and history—were waning by 1985. First, in an era of ubiquitous air travel, transportation no longer imposed much of a burden on teams. Teams took busses, once the primary form of travel, only for games within an hour or two of the home campus. Anything further and the athletic department would spring for a flight. With airplanes now the main transit method, it made little difference whether the opposition campus was 200 or 2000 miles away; only a few hours at most would be added to the itinerary. Michigan spent a week traveling to California for the Rose Bowl in 1901. The same trip by the Wolverines in 1990 took six hours from doorstep to hotel.

Second, the television revolution brought about by *NCAA v. University of Oklahoma* transformed overlapping geography and nearby fan bases within a conference from a benefit into a hindrance. Recall that prior to the 1984 Supreme Court decision, only the NCAA negotiated television contracts, with a few limited exceptions. After the Court held that a continuation of the NCAA's policy would violate antitrust laws, the teams gave their negotiating authority to their conferences, and the conferences then shopped their slates of conference games to television networks.

Before 1984, the most important factor for a game to reach television was its national relevance, since only a couple of games were shown at a time due to NCAA restrictions. A chosen game would be broadcast to almost the entire country, so that game had to appeal to as many viewers as possible. After 1984 and the Supreme Court decision, television networks were blessed with an abundance of games from which to choose, since the conferences could now sell however many contests they wished. Because of that glut of programming, the networks chose their programming not based on which games would hold the most attention nationwide, but based on which games could gain the most attention in each of the major markets.

For example, suppose that the most popular match nationally on a particular week is that between Texas and Oklahoma. If a television network could choose only one game, it would choose that one. No matter how popular that game is nationally, however, there are particular markets in which other games would be more popular with the local population. Fans in the South might prefer to watch Georgia and Auburn; those along the Pacific coast might prefer USC and Washington. Because after 1984 the networks could air more contests, the most valuable games were not those with broad national appeal, but those with extremely strong local and regional appeal. Better to show five games to twenty-million viewers than one game to ten-million viewers, even if each of the five games earned only four-million viewers apiece.

Under the joint NCAA contracts, conferences needed teams with strong national appeal. Now, the strongest conferences were those that controlled the most major television markets. Mid-level teams became more valuable, as long as those teams carried sizeable fan bases in major cities. A conference like the SWC, which was located almost entirely within Texas, found itself with few major markets and a couple of areas where there was almost *too* much interest. Conversely, the Big Ten now controlled Chicago, Detroit, Cleveland, Cincinnati, Minneapolis, Indianapolis, and Milwaukee, not to mention the campus towns of the individual schools.

The logic of expansion was now irreversibly altered. When the Pac-8 expanded in 1978 (while still under the NCAA television contract regime), the conference added Arizona and Arizona State, whose campuses are only one-hundred miles or so apart. Adding just one of those teams would likely have earned Arizona's major television markets for the Pac-8, but this was not yet the conference's concern, since the Pac-8 was not the entity selling games to television networks. A decade later, two schools in a sparsely populated state felt like overkill, especially since ten teams instead of nine would now split the television revenue.

An even more egregious example of market oversaturation was the SWC's adoption of Houston in 1976. The SWC was already the prime attraction in the Houston market, regardless of the Cougars' success as an independent. Texas and Texas A&M alone—with a tiny bit of help from local Rice—ensured that Houstonians were fully invested in the SWC. But the addition of Houston was not meant to increase the conference's popularity within Texas, which was ironclad. Instead, the addition of Houston might persuade the networks to play a couple more SWC games nationally during the course of the season, such as when the Cougars played Texas or Arkansas.

But in the post-*NCAA v. University of Oklahoma* world, Houston provided the SWC with slight benefit. If Houston (and Rice, and Baylor) seceded from the SWC, television networks would still not hesitate to broadcast Texas vs. Texas A&M in every market in the state. Houston provided nothing the SWC did not already have, and even worse for the other SWC teams, the Cougars athletic department now earned a portion of the shared television revenue.

It is almost impossible to overstate the effects of the revised television regime on the concept of the modern football conference. Teams have always competed against one another off and on the field. Failing to keep up with your competitors in revenue leads to declines in the quality of coaches hired and facilities built (and recruits bought, if you want to be cynical). But now the parameters of the off-field game had changed. Teams belonging to those conferences suddenly disadvantaged by their geography or by unproductive members were now threatened, as rivals from across the nation used their superior positions with respect to television to increase revenue at the expense of the programs shackled to unfruitful relationships.

A few years passed before anyone fully realized just how much the Supreme Court ruling had changed matters. The immediate effect of the decision was that prices for games fell severely. As games flooded the market, networks played teams and conferences off against one another in an effort to procure the best deal for themselves. For the first couple of seasons under the new system, schools had little time to worry about much besides merely keeping their heads above water.

Fortunately for athletic departments, the rising supply of games was accompanied by rising demand for those games. For one thing, the bigger menu of games each weekend probably made college football a more popular sport overall, though this is difficult to prove. More importantly, the expansion of cable television—and the Entertainment and Sports Programming Network ("ESPN") in particular—introduced competition on the other side of the negotiating table, which in turn drove prices for college football games back up. ESPN was the first national 24-hour sports network, and its all-sports-all-the-time focus left the station with lots of inventory to fill.

In many ways, ESPN fueled the larger cable television phenomenon. Sports fans could now watch games they could not have seen before without going to the stadium. This newfound freedom proved intoxicating. Many viewers subscribed to cable only for ESPN and other sports channels. Because of this popularity, ESPN could charge cable companies with hefty carriage rates (the fee that cable companies pay to the networks to carry their stations). Between 1981 and 1986, for example, ESPN's carriage rate increased nine-fold. Cable companies could not refuse these high rates because so much of its consumer base existed only because they offered ESPN; without ESPN, cable companies would lose these customers entirely.

Nor were carriage rates the only source of revenue for the network—indeed, they made up only about 40 percent of what ESPN earned each year. Because the demographic watching ESPN was overwhelmingly male and middle class—i.e. the demographic advertisers covet most, since that group is responsible for the spending decisions in many households—advertising rates were much higher than the average for cable stations with similar ratings. Flush with advertising and carriage-rate cash, ESPN offered bigger contracts for college football games, which in turn forced the national networks to either sweeten their own deals or risk losing their college football programming to cable.

With money now trickling back into the television market, the jostling between conferences for lucrative deals intensified, and the logic of the new television market became clear. Just as always, conferences hoped to strengthen their on-field product; fans have always preferred watching good games to bad ones. But fans also prefer watching local games, all else being equal. The trick for conference commissioners was to find teams that could both strengthen their product and, at the same time, package more eyeballs to the television networks.

This singular focus on television revenue undercut the final rationale of conferences. Many of the major conferences had bonded over some critical event in college football's history: fights over amateurism, or postseason play, or athletic scholarships. Those wars forged alliances stronger than mere self-interest would suggest. Suddenly, these common experiences counted for little.

New fault lines fissured previously unbroken ground. The recombinations fashioned in conformity with the new economic realities of the sport would be rooted primarily in economic self-interest.

***

The football program of that small Catholic school in rural Indiana was, by 1990, the most valuable commodity in college sports. Perhaps unique amongst college football teams, Notre Dame had a truly national following. Decades of success helped, as did the Fighting Irish's propensity for traveling from coast to coast to play games of national importance. Notre Dame's reputation as the national face of Catholicism in America did not hurt, either, and this in-road with America's religious plurality moved television dials in cities with major Catholic populations across the country.

Put another way, Notre Dame was the only school that bucked the localization trend begun by the Supreme Court. Rather than contributing a major television network or two completely, Notre Dame captured a significant percentage of fans in dozens of markets. Many people hated the Fighting Irish because of this omnipresence, but even that hatred was a good thing as far as networks were concerned; if people are watching your games, it doesn't really matter whether they are hoping you lose or praying you win.

Following the *NCAA v. University of Oklahoma* decision, the CFA earned the right to negotiate television contracts on behalf of its member schools, much like the NCAA had done prior to the decision. By banding together, the CFA hoped it might avoid the worst effects of competition by presenting a united front to the television networks. Yet as successful as the CFA had been in court, it was a disaster as a negotiating entity. All of the problems the NCAA faced while negotiating national contracts reappeared when the CFA took over the job. The conferences within the organization distrusted one another, and the more popular programs fought for a larger share of the revenue each time a new television contract was negotiated. Smaller CFA schools resented these money grabs, but in truth those small schools benefitted the most under the CFA arrangement; never would they earn as much individually as they could when paired with the stalwarts of the sport.

Given its national popularity, and its newfound freedom to convert that popularity into television revenue, it was only a matter of time before Notre Dame abandoned the CFA. In February 1990, NBC offered — and the Fighting Irish accepted — a $38 million deal covering five seasons, the first national television network arrangement directly with a school since Penn's contract with ABC in 1950. Whether Notre Dame was seduced by NBC — as NBC had tried to seduce the CFA back in 1981, thus setting off the television crisis in the first place — or whether Notre Dame went out on its own looking for an independent television contract is a matter of some conjecture still today. The school maintained that NBC simply an offer it couldn't refuse, while the other members of the CFA were unsurprisingly skeptical by Notre Dame's claim to virginal innocence.

The truth is probably somewhere in the middle, and even if it isn't — even if Notre Dame were wholly innocent or wholly guilty — the subsequent reality would not be changed. For the first time, an individual program accepted an offer from a national network to televise every home game across the country. Notre Dame earned millions of dollars more under the NBC contract than it could have hoped to earn under the auspices of the CFA. Given that the CFA had been formed to maximize revenue, its remaining schools could not complain too vigorously when Notre Dame pursued that same goal in a different manner.

In response to the loss of Notre Dame, ABC — which had reached an agreement with the CFA just two weeks prior to NBC-Notre Dame announcement — cut its contract payout to the CFA by $25 million. With the defection of one school, the 62-member organization lost over 10 percent of its value. However outraged CFA members might have been by the duplicity, this was how the battles of college football would henceforth be fought. Conference commissioners, athletic directors, and university presidents— overwhelmingly a savvy lot where their self-interest is at stake— now understood the rules of the new game they were playing. After decades of inactivity, the pieces began to move once more around the chessboard.

Independence

Penn State president Bryce Jordan placed a call to fellow university president Stanley Ikenberry of Illinois in late 1989. Ikenberry had been a professor at Penn State before accepting the Illinois presidency in 1979, and though his tenure in State College did not overlap with Jordan's, Ikenberry was the closest connection the Pennsylvania school had to the Big Ten.

Eight years before, Penn State had tried to fashion a football conference out of the schools of the Northeast, the strongest remaining bastion of independence. The project was ill-conceived. The two best of the few powerful football programs in the area — Syracuse and Boston College — had recently helped found the Big East, a basketball-centric arrangement that allowed those schools to retain their independence in football. Just two years into their relationship, neither Boston College nor Syracuse was willing to leave. A handful of other strong teams in the area — Pittsburgh, maybe West Virginia — might be convinced to join, but the rest of the conference would consist of the low-level patsies that littered the region. Despite the best efforts of Penn State head coach Joe Paterno, the "Northeast Conference" concept fell through.

The next year, the Big East revived the idea, in a way. Although the Big East was a basketball conference, and Penn State had little success in basketball, Big East commissioner Dave Gavitt approached Paterno with the idea of Penn State joining the conference. This would allow the Nittany Lions to retain their independence in college football, maintain flexibility in scheduling fellow Northeastern schools, and find a home for Penn State's non-revenue sports.

But Gavitt had outrun the support of his schools. Syracuse and Boston College, the two Division 1-A football programs in the Big

East, were supportive of Penn State's addition, but several of the basketball-only schools did not see the reasoning behind adding a football school to a conference that did not play football. If anything, Penn State would dilute the quality of play in basketball while creating extra headaches about how the Big East should split its revenue between football-playing teams and the others. Six votes in favor were needed to invite Penn State; only five votes in favor were cast. Penn State would instead join the Eastern 8 Conference for non-revenue sports, and the Big East safeguarded its basketball purity.

Now, almost a decade and two football national championships later, president Jordan was preparing for the future of Penn State. Paterno had been head coach for 23 years and was now 62 years old; at most, Jordan figured, Paterno had five or so more years left as head of the program. Under Paterno's direction, Penn State scaled its way to the peak of college football, but there was no guarantee it would remain there after Paterno's retirement. A stable relationship in the Big Ten would insure against such misfortune.

The move to the Big Ten made sense from the academic side as well. Each Big Ten school was a member of the Association of American Universities ("AAU"), a collection of elite research schools; Penn State was also an AAU member. Each Big Ten school housed significant graduate-level research programs, just as Penn State did. These research programs earned the institutions tens of millions of dollars apiece in grant money from the federal government. That money was then shared through the Committee for Institutional Cooperation ("CIC"), an association of the ten conference schools plus original Big Ten member University of Chicago.

The CIC relationship was not much different than the Big Ten's athletic relationship. Each new CIC member would be another mouth to feed, with the new school's research programs earning a share of the CIC's funds. But bringing on a top-tier research school would contribute to the funds of the overall whole, just as adding a top-tier football program would add to the revenue of all Big Ten schools. And most importantly, the CIC—like conference athletic revenue—was not zero-sum. The combination of research teams across schools made it more likely that those schools could access federal research grants, which would thereby benefit all schools in the CIC.

Ikenberry was receptive to Jordan's overtures, and told Jordan he would present the idea of expansion to the other Big Ten presidents. The academic leaders at the remaining nine schools were likewise interested in Penn State's addition to the CIC, while Big Ten commissioner Jim Delany approved of the expansion on the athletic side of things. With little prior fanfare and total silence in the media prior to the announcement, the Big Ten presidents unanimously approved Penn State in late 1989 as the future eleventh team in the conference, and the first new team in four decades.

There was only one problem: no one had told the athletic directors, who revolted upon hearing the news. Bo Schembechler, long-time head coach at Michigan and athletic director at that school when the Penn State announcement was made, carried on in the tradition of Fielding Yost and threw a tantrum at the prospect of expansion. Even more so, he resented the encroachment upon what he saw as the athletic department's turf:

> I think there is a buddy system, and that's how it happened. All of a sudden, the [presidents] tender Penn State an invitation and [Penn State] accepts and then they dump it into the laps of the athletic administrators and say "work it out." [...] It kind of tells you the prestige of the position of athletic director. [...] Historically, the presidents and faculty representatives dominate the Big Ten Conference and down here somewhere is the athletic director. He's counting the pencils and paper clips; stuff like that. That's a sad

commentary. […] In the next five years, the presidents will completely confuse intercollegiate athletics. It will be in some kind of a mess and in about 1995, they'll dump it on the athletic directors and say, "you straighten this thing out," and we might be back to normal by about the year 2000.

Schembechler was not alone in his indignation. Bobby Knight, head coach of the Indiana men's basketball team, resented having to go "camping" in central Pennsylvania each season. Several football coaches privately bristled at the addition of another likely loss to the schedule each season. To Paterno, Jordan, and the rest of the Penn State administration, the episode was a public replay of the Big East's rejection of the Nittany Lions back in 1982.

Cooler heads prevailed in the end. Penn State's move to the Big Ten made too much sense to be rejected. Where coaches saw the distance between State College and the other Big Ten campuses as a negative, most athletic directors soon realized that an expansion into Pennsylvania gained the Big Ten access into households across the Mid-Atlantic. After given a few weeks to calm down, the athletic directors were provided an opportunity to vote on Penn State's inclusion in the club. The vote was unanimous, as it had been for the presidents, save for Indiana. A few weeks' time was hardly sufficient to dampen the anger of Bobby Knight.

***

Further south, athletic directors had been exploring their options for quite some time. The SEC was the most selective club in college football. Since its secession from the Southern Conference in 1932, the SEC had not admitted a new member. Instead, the originally thirteen-team SEC gradually shed its weakest programs—Sewanee in 1940, Georgia Tech in 1964, and Tulane in 1966—making it the only major conference to shrink between its inception and the 1980s.

But circumstances had changed. Despite the relative paucity of major television markets in the South, the SEC encompassed the most valuable real estate in college football. Long shunned by professional leagues, southern sports fans had no choice but to turn to the local universities for their allegiances.

That ferocity served the conference well before and after the Supreme Court's decision in *NCAA v. University of Oklahoma*. Before the Court struck down the NCAA's national television contract, SEC teams earned their national television appearances through the strength of their most powerful programs, the teams that the entire nation tuned in to watch on Saturdays. After the Supreme Court gave conferences the power to negotiate their own television contracts, the CFA negotiated on behalf of the SEC and other major conferences, minus the Big Ten and Pac-10. SEC teams exploited their position as the most popular conference to arrange better deals for itself within the CFA's revenue-sharing plan. The CFA's other conferences had little choice but to accede to the increasingly unequal division, lest the SEC seek its own deal alone.

This power was an aphrodisiac to non-SEC teams no longer satisfied with their own situations. For their part, SEC leaders knew they likely could have their pick of suitors should they decide to wed. But while the SEC slowly explored its options, the Big Ten presidents were approving Penn State's invitation. Suddenly, a process that SEC leaders assumed they would dictate felt outside of their control.

The SEC's concern was not that the Big Ten has stolen a potential target. Penn State would never have joined the SEC or even have been a serious contender to do so; geography still counted for something, and the cultural differences between the Pennsylvania school and the Midwestern Big Ten would have been multiplied tenfold with the SEC. More concerning was that other, closer targets might grow tired of waiting for the SEC's invitation, instead pairing with other conferences while the SEC's power eroded.

***

The obvious questions for the SEC were "who" and "how many?" Before 1990, ten was seen as the unofficial natural limit on conference size. The only precedent for larger arrangements had been the Southern Conference, which split apart twice—once spawning the SEC, the next time the ACC—because of its unwieldy size. Even ten teams required some compromises. Because football teams were limited to eight conference games per season, every team in a ten-team conference would miss one team each season. Every additional team beyond ten meant an additional missed matchup per team.

Another difficulty with expansion became colorfully known as the "corncob" problem. Professional leagues do a variety of things—rookie drafts, salary caps, weighted scheduling—to give teams at the bottom a boost. College football is not so forgiving. Every year, the ten teams of the SEC played eight conference games apiece, and every year, those teams won forty games and lost forty games. For every powerful team you added to the mix (the kernels), there had to be another program at the base supplying those wins (the cob). Every Alabama needed a Mississippi State, every Tennessee a Vanderbilt.

Yet despite the danger of overloading the conference with too much quality, the SEC was not interested in adding another Vanderbilt or Mississippi State. Each new team would earn a share of the SEC's revenue. Readmitting Tulane might give seven or eight current SEC teams an extra win each year, but Tulane would also suck away one-eleventh of the SEC's revenue.

The Big Ten had solved this problem, accidentally, when the presidents largely bypassed the athletic directors. Ohio State's biology department was not worried that too much success at Penn State would somehow detract from their own efforts. The coaches complained when they learned of the invitation, but by that point, it was too late.

Conversely, SEC expansion was driven by its athletic departments. Those athletic departments hoped to create a richer, stronger SEC, but not at the expense of their own programs. Schools preferred admission of the strongest programs possible, as long as those teams were far away from their campus. Thus the western half of the SEC looked to Florida 0State and Miami as new members, while Georgia and especially Florida resisted the inclusion of those teams, fearing for their positions in the new SEC with powerful rivals so close. The western schools, for their part, were not excited about an SEC with Texas or Texas A&M.

As newspapers mentioned each new scenario, speculation grew, almost as though the teams cited by the journalists were not possibilities, but inevitabilities. Imagine, an SEC with fourteen, sixteen, even eighteen teams! Surely the other conferences would respond in turn. No doubt the Big Ten would grow, despite assurances from Ikenberry and Delany that the conference was not looking to add members; eleven was too awkward a number to stick for long. And if expansion to sixteen teams was inevitable, which conferences would fail to meet their quota?

***

Six independent teams won national championships during the 1980s. Within five years, independence in college football was practically extinct.

The culprit, as with so much else, was *NCAA v. University of Oklahoma*. Before that decision, the key to getting on television was national popularity. Networks only showed a couple of games per week, so television appearances were limited mostly to teams with broad-based appeal. Independence did not hamper such appeal. In fact, it could contribute to it, especially if it allowed a team to break the chains of college football's regionalism, as Notre Dame had done in the 1910s and 1920s.

With the explosion in games available to networks after 1984, however, local popularity mattered as much—perhaps more—than national popularity. Penn State won two national championships during the 1980s while independent, and that success ensured plenty of television placement outside of State College, Pennsylvania. But that kind of success is not everlasting, and should the program hit a snag, those national television appearances would disappear. And the State College television market alone was not large enough to support 28 sports.

Penn State was hardly alone in this predicament; Miami, Florida State, Syracuse, Virginia Tech, and all other independent teams faced the same problem. In a world where local television markets counted for so much, a team's fortunes could rise and fall dramatically within the span of a couple of years. With a bad season or two, those national appearances would disappear, which meant less money, which in turn meant further irrelevancy.

The CFA, in theory, was supposed to ensure against such wild swings by roughly duplicating what the NCAA had previously done. But the CFA was already fraying by 1990. Teams that were more popular sought larger payouts, which undercut the insurance function the CFA was supposed to provide. Only conferences—those safe, stable, almost timeless conferences—provided the financial protection sought by the independent programs.

Happy football programs are all alike; unhappy football programs are each unhappy in their own way. Dissatisfaction with independence was nearly universal, but each bachelor program had different concerns about their coming marriages. The spinsters at the bottom—the Southwestern Louisianas, Northern Illinoises, and other directional-school misfits—worried about finding any partners at all. Those schools were already on the wrong side of independence, shut out of television and with little hope of advancement. Without conference affiliation, those schools might be unable to remain part of Division I-A.

At the far other end of the spectrum, the most attractive independent teams—Penn State, Miami, Notre Dame, Florida State—could be sure that their specific concerns would be addressed before hitching themselves to a conference. There was undoubtedly some concern at those schools about waiting too long or missing an opportunity. But those teams could also play their suitors off against one another, thereby procuring the best deals possible for themselves. And under no circumstances would Miami or Florida State be left out in the cold.

Then there were the teams in the middle, who didn't quite know where they fit. Take Louisville, for example: historically one of the better programs in college basketball, but not a traditional football power (though ranked #14 in the nation to finish the 1990 season), and located within a reasonably sized television market. Was Louisville more like Florida State or Northern Illinois? For how long could a team like Louisville hold out for the best possible deal?

***

Independence was not the only arrangement outliving its usefulness. Down in the Lone Star State, the Southwest Conference was staggering through its final, gruesome years.

The causes of death were multiple. Cause one: lack of parity. Either Texas, Arkansas, or Texas A&M finished every season from 1985 onwards with the best record in the SWC. Upon returning from their two-year death penalty, SMU won only three conference games over the next seven seasons. Rice went 5–25 from 1987 through 1990. TCU finished only one season after 1984 over .500 in conference play (a 4–3 record in 1994). With so many free bingo squares for the most powerful teams, fans lost interest in the SWC.

Cause two: endless scandals. In the SWC's final decade of existence, four of the nine programs spent at least one season ineligible for the conference championship. Houston's 1989 team featured a Heisman Trophy winner in Andre Ware and was the first small-school SWC program to win six conference games since Baylor in 1986. The Cougars followed that up with an even better 1990 campaign, going 7–1, the last team in the SWC besides Texas and Texas A&M to win seven conference games in a season. Yet none of that mattered, because Houston was suspended from bowl games by the NCAA and was ineligible to win the SWC championship both years. In 1994, Texas A&M went undefeated in conference play, but, once again because of NCAA penalties, could not win the crown. The disaster at SMU need not be recounted here. With so many lost seasons, fans had less incentive to watch.

Cause three: too much geographic overlap. Eight teams in the same state was overkill, even a state as big, populous, and football-crazy as Texas. Once you left Texas's borders, few people were much interested in the SWC's affairs. Once again, the lack of parity and the low quality of play didn't help, either, but even had the SWC performed much better during the 1980s and early 1990s, it would have been difficult to overcome being so condensed in a limited area.

As with the independent schools, not all of the SWC teams could be optimistic about landing on their feet. There would always be a place for Texas, Arkansas, and Texas A&M, and all three teams were linked to discussions with the SEC. If the move to fourteen-team or sixteen-team conferences really was imminent, perhaps all three of the SWC's major powers could remain united. But the other SWC programs understood there would not be enough lifeboats onboard the sinking ship. SMU was a rotting husk of its former self, ravaged by the NCAA's death penalty. Rice had been uncompetitive for so long that President Kennedy was making cracks about the Owls during speeches in the 1960s. Either the SWC would be salvaged, or those teams would cease playing major conference college football.

***

Meanwhile, the SEC dithered. In May 1989—seven months before the Big Ten announced its invitation to Penn State—the SEC announced that it was investigating the possibility of expansion. A year later, the conference didn't know much more than what it knew when it made the announcement. SWC teams were dissatisfied. Independent teams felt financially insecure. None of this was breaking news.

But disagreements within the SEC stalled progress. The two major independent schools under consideration, Miami and Florida State, were unacceptable to Florida. Under no circumstances would the Gator athletic department allow nearby rivals access to the nation's most popular athletic conference. Maybe the rest of the conference could win that battle and override Florida's veto, but the battle would still have to be fought, and internecine fights like those were always messy. Better to move on to other targets, for the time being.

More agreeable to Florida, and almost as agreeable to the rest of the conference, was the trio of SWC powers looking for safety. The Texas television markets, insufficient though they may have been by themselves, would be quite a boon to the already-popular SEC. Snagging the University of Texas alone would likely gain entry into both Dallas and Houston most weekends, and Texas A&M might do the trick as well. The problem, however, was that plenty of powerful people in Texas were unwilling to see the two teams split up. Adding Texas *and* Texas A&M meant either that the SEC would be foreclosed from adding Florida State or Miami, or that the conference would jump from ten to at least thirteen—probably at least fourteen—teams. Best to wait on that decision, too.

The last of the unsatisfied SWC troika, Arkansas, posed no such problems. Arkansas was competitive—but not too competitive, not competitive enough to force one of the current

SEC schools into the cob. Arkansas was close enough to make transportation easy, but far enough away that new, untapped television markets came available. The Arkansas legislature would not hold up the exit of the Razorbacks from the SWC in return for some other, undeserving team receiving a golden parachute as well. And if not exactly a home run, landing Arkansas was at least a solid single, with more batters yet to come to the plate for the SEC.

There was little doubt that Arkansas would accept an SEC invitation if offered. The Razorbacks would earn about $1 million more each season in the SEC than the SWC. Arkansas already had a longstanding rivalry with the SEC's Mississippi, a connection to their new home that Penn State could not boast with regards to the Big Ten. It was doubtful the SWC would survive for another decade, and while Arkansas was a good program, it sat in a less-advantageous position than the major Texas schools. Better to get out first and have a guaranteed place at the premier conference in college football than stay committed to a decaying arrangement for too long.

Nevertheless, even with the obvious benefits to both sides, the process dragged out over the course of the summer of 1990. The Big Ten had the benefit of catching everyone off-guard—including several of its athletic directors—when it announced its invitation to Penn State. The SEC had no such luxury, and its leaders watched the entire process unfold in the newspapers. SWC athletic directors pleaded with Arkansas to stick with their conference, citing the added travel in the SEC (as though coming into Texas for every match was convenient) and loyalty (as though those schools would do anything differently if circumstances were changed). Journalists fantasized about the coming revolution, wherein the SEC's expansion would set in motion a process that would end with Kansas and Colorado sharing a conference with Penn State and Syracuse.

Finally, in late July, the Alabama Journal newspaper announced that a decision had been made. Arkansas and Florida State had accepted invitations to join the SEC.

***

Less than half of the report was true. The SEC had indeed invited Arkansas to join, and although Arkansas would soon accept the invitation, it had not yet officially done so. It wasn't Pulitzer-grade work, but the Atlanta Journal had at least gotten the Arkansas part mostly right.

It was also true that the SEC had voted to expand the conference by two teams at a time. NCAA regulations allowed conferences of twelve teams or more to play conference championship games at the end of the regular season. Adding that one game to the schedule would likely earn the SEC millions of dollars in revenue.

But the SEC had not extended an invitation to Florida State. For one thing, there was the Florida problem; with the Gators' approval unattainable, eight of the nine remaining conference schools would have to approve Florida State as SEC-member number twelve. There was no such overwhelming support for any one team when so many free-agent programs were available. More importantly, though, the SEC did not invite Florida State because the SEC could not be sure the Seminoles would accept the invitation.

The threat of rejection was very real, the SEC's economic superiority notwithstanding. First, as in the Big Ten, the athletic department would not be the sole decisionmaker in Tallahassee. Five of the eight ACC schools belonged to the prestigious Association of American Universities, while only two of the ten SEC schools belonged to that club. The ACC did not have a similar setup as the Big Ten with the CIC, but the faculty at Florida State (which did not belong to the AAU) preferred the bump in stature that came from the improvement in academic peers.

Jealousy undoubtedly also played a role. Florida State was a women's college until 1947, and the SEC itself—not to mention the programs within the SEC—predated the Seminoles football program by fourteen years. SEC programs happily scheduled Florida State during the Seminoles' lean early years, but matches were harder to arrange as Bill Peterson and Bobby Bowden built the program upward from the foundations. Bowden in particular, who had coached Florida State since the mid-1970s, resented the change in attitude within the SEC as the Seminoles developed into one of the elite independent programs in the nation. These petty historical squabbles could be overcome, but they were obstacles.

Florida State had "corncob" concerns of its own. Every week in the powerful SEC would be a challenge, and the Seminoles were committed to playing rival Miami each year out-of-conference. The ruthless, zero-sum reality was that some team would get worse with Florida State's arrival, and it was by no means clear that Florida State could avoid being that team.

Finally, the economic landscape in 1990 was not necessarily the same as what the economic landscape would be in 2000 or 2020. The hordes of devoted southern college football fans did enhance the SEC's negotiating position with television networks, but if you squinted hard enough, you could see some problems for the conference on the horizon. There were only a handful of major television markets in the Deep South, and the states in that region were relatively depopulated. Once upon a time, professional leagues had shied away from the South for that reason, but the NFL, MLB, and NBA all now had teams in SEC states, and professional teams might sap enthusiasm for the college game over time. Harvard, Yale, Fordham, and Penn had all enjoyed their time in the sun; conferences similarly waxed and waned. The trick for Florida State would be finding the next great conference, not the current great one.

If not the SEC, then where? One possibility was the Metro Conference, to which Florida State already belonged. The Metro Conference was not a football conference, but the independent football programs that made up the Metro Conference faced the same predicament as Florida State. As the name suggested, the Metro Conference already had inroads in many reasonably sized cities; a conference could do a lot worse than teams in New Orleans (Tulane), Louisville, Memphis, and Cincinnati.

The rest of the Metro Conference was arriving at the same conclusion, and shortly after Penn State's departure to the Big Ten, the conference commissioned a report from Raycom Sports on whether moving into football would be feasible. The answer was yes, and resoundingly so, especially if the conference quickly seized the initiative. Not only should the eight-team Metro Conference add football, the Raycom report said, but it should enter the expansion game itself. If the Metro Conference could convince the remaining major independent teams to join—Miami, West Virginia, a few teams from the similarly basketball-dependent Big East—it could become a superconference of its own. Moreover, it could be a superconference covering approximately 35 percent of the nation's television markets, more than twice as much coverage as the SEC could provide.

This move would be radical—too radical, in fact, for the athletic departments currently inhabiting the Metro Conference. When the conference had been formed in the 1970s, those schools were merely looking for a convenient place to stick their basketball teams and non-revenue sports. Less than twenty years later, Raycom was saying that not only should the schools chose the Metro Conference over those conferences that had been playing football for decades, but also that the Metro Conference should double in size. However much economic sense the plan may have made, there were too many moving parts for the plan to be successful.

Without the SEC or the Metro Conference, Florida State's options were running out. The Big East—a similar arrangement to the Metro Conference centered in the Northeast—was reportedly also making a run at expanding to football, but that move would, if anything, make less sense than the Metro Conference conversion. Most of the teams in the Big East didn't even play Division I-A football, so significant expansion was needed to hit the realistic minimum of teams needed to create a football conference. The SWC was hardly a decent option for Florida State after the departure of Arkansas. And nearly everyone else—the Pac-10, Big Eight, and Big Ten—was too far away.

All this makes it sound like the ACC was the only realistic option, or worse, a destination of last resort for Florida State. But the ACC had real advantages: proximity, academics, a quickly growing population base, and a soft schedule for continuing domination. The money wouldn't be much different from what the Seminoles would earn from the SEC; in fact, with the ACC's uneven revenue sharing, Florida State might earn more money in the ACC. By mid-September 1990—two months after the Alabama Journal article erroneously sending Florida State to the SEC was printed—the decision was made. The Seminoles were ACC-bound.

***

With Florida State gone and the Texas schools so closely bonded to one another—whether by choice or otherwise—the SEC was running out of options.

The biggest independent prize remaining was Miami, winner of three national championships during the 1980s. Undeniably successful, the Hurricanes were a peculiar case in almost all respects. Not long before, Miami football was an afterthought in Southern Florida, and the Miami administration had considered demoting the program to Division I-AA or abandoning football outright as recently as the late 1970s.

Such thoughts were crazy by 1990. During the decade between the Miami football program's brush with suicide and their third national championship in 1989, "The U" was one of the most identifiable—and valuable—brands in college sports.

But Miami's popularity was not an unalloyed positive. Part of its allure stemmed from the program's brazenness and outright disrespect for opponents and the rules. Many believed—accurately—that Miami was ignoring NCAA regulations, and that a SMU-type situation could unfold at any moment. (A few years later, things got so bad in Miami that Sports Illustrated would run as its cover, in simple white letters against a green background with no illustration, the words "Why the University of Miami should drop football.") Miami's success was undeniable, however, and kids across the country were wearing Miami gear, where less than a generation ago few people would have even been able to identify the team colors.

Miami, much like Florida State, had concerns about the SEC. The SEC schedule might prove too difficult, and with Miami committed to playing Florida State annually, the road to future national championships might be impassible in the SEC. Also, strangely for a school so far south, a great deal of Miami's alumni base lived in the Midwest and Northeast. Where Miami as an independent could play Notre Dame, Boston College, and other independent schools, those rivalries would mostly disappear should they join a southern conference.

Seven-hundred miles up the Orange Blossom Railroad, the University of South Carolina had no such qualms about SEC membership. Dreams of a football Metro Conference died with Florida State's departure to the ACC, depriving the Metro Conference of its most significant football asset. South Carolina's relationship with the ACC was chilly at best—the Gamecocks had left the conference in 1971, and Clemson had some of the same concerns with readmission that Florida had with Florida State's admission to the SEC—so the ACC was not a preferred option for South Carolina.

Moreover, South Carolina knew that it had probably been option number six for the SEC when the conference began investigating expansion in 1989. Things had fallen into place perfectly for South Carolina, and the Gamecocks program could not quibble about worries as insignificant as schedule strength or travel concerns.

***

Further north, the Big East watched the picking apart of the Metro Conference and wondered whether it might be next. The Big Ten sat, surely discontented, at an ominous eleven teams, with Penn State rival Pittsburgh already inside the conference's geographic footprint, and with Syracuse not too much further away. Only three of the nine Big East schools played Division I-A college football, but losing any one of those three would severely cripple the conference, and losing all three would likely destroy it.

The non-football schools—St. John's, Providence, Villanova, Georgetown, Connecticut, and Seton Hall—were the confounding variables. To the majority of the conference's membership, the Big East was a basketball conference only, and perhaps the greatest basketball conference ever created. Any move that deemphasized basketball in favor of football would hurt those six non-football schools. They would gain nothing if the Big East added football, since basketball revenue would then be split with worse programs, while football revenue remained entirely in the wallets of the football schools.

NCAA rules required at least four teams to make a conference, but the Big East would probably need at least eight teams to credibly compete for television contracts. For the Big East to reach eight football teams, five additional football programs were needed. Adding five new full members, however, would increase the basketball membership to fourteen. Several of the added schools would be worthless to the basketball members, which would see important rivalries diluted.

Thus Mike Tranghese, commissioner of the Big East, announced quite bluntly in October 1990 that he was "opposed to" the option of adding five additional programs, even if expansion was necessary to keep the three football programs within the Big East. But what other options might there be? Syracuse, Pittsburgh, and Boston College remaining independent "[didn't] solve the problem," as Tranghese admitted. And the other options were outlandish at best. Tranghese floated the idea of a football-only merger with the ACC, but was rebuffed; adopting the Big East's football membership wholesale would foreclose the ACC from being more discriminating should future expansion opportunities appear. Similar mergers with the SWC and Big Eight were likewise floated in internal Big East meetings, but these ideas were even more ridiculous than the proposed ACC merger. Syracuse was no more interested in playing road games at SMU or Rice than Texas was.

Expansion it was, then, no matter how unwilling the basketball schools may have been. The disbandment of the Big East, after all, would have been far worse for their programs than the addition of a few weak teams to the conference.

First order of business was convincing Miami to join, which at this point would not be too difficult. The SEC had already moved on to South Carolina, and the Big East could offer the Hurricanes regular access to the Northeast, something no other major conference could do. Miami was essential to the Big East's expansion plan, since the Hurricanes were the most significant remaining major independent team (besides Notre Dame). And with The U on board, the Big East might just convince enough others to join to make the project feasible.

Despite the ACC and SEC getting first pick, there was no shortage of independents available. There was the rest of the

Metro Conference for starters, six members of which remained unattached. Not all of them would make good candidates— Memphis and Tulane were not getting invitations under any circumstances—but a couple of them were viable additions. Virginia Tech and Louisville, for example, had respectable football programs, and Southern Mississippi was at least plausible as a new member. West Virginia, another strong independent program from the Atlantic 10, would likewise add to the quality of play.

Expansion decisions could not be made entirely on strength of play, though. The need for television contracts dictated that the Big East pack as many major markets into the new football conference as possible. Boston, Pittsburgh, and Miami were a great start, but most of the best football programs still available fell in rural areas.

After Miami, the four remaining Big East invitations were split cleanly between the two needs. Two of the four invitations would go to strong football programs—West Virginia and Virginia Tech—in order to improve the quality of play. The remaining two invitations were given to patsies in major metropolitan areas: Temple in Philadelphia, and Rutgers in the New York City metro area. As a sop to the Providences and Seton Halls of the conference, the four invitations would be for football only; the Big East would not expand in basketball. The conference became a Venn diagram with football programs in one circle, basketball programs in another, and a small overlapping circle of dual-sport schools in the middle.

The invited schools accepted the Big East's invitations with little fuss. The pressures of maintaining an independent football program were never higher, and these schools had already been passed over by the SEC and ACC. When times were good, independent teams could keep bowl payouts and television contracts for themselves. When times were bad and money scarce, the rest of the athletic department felt the pinch, since football was responsible for paying the bills. Big East football—inconceivable in

1989, a longshot as late as October 1990—was a reality by the 1991 season.

***

Broken, bloodied, but somehow still breathing, the SWC survived the departure of Arkansas in 1990 (effective for the 1992 season). Karma intervened and punished Arkansas with a 6–10 record in its final two SWC seasons, worse than Houston, Baylor, and TCU over that period, and only one game better than Rice. The schadenfreude at Arkansas's collapse was a hollow, empty pleasure, but the athletic departments of the SWC underclass would take their chuckles whatever way they could get them during such trying times.

For the next three years, nearly every imaginable option and combination was pursued by one school or another in an attempt to either save the SWC or save themselves. At the bottom of the conference, the choices were few. After being arm-twisted into remaining with the SWC by politicians, Texas and Texas A&M fired a warning shot at the remainder of the conference: the leading pair would no longer continue carrying the rest of the conference by themselves. If the SWC were to survive, the smaller schools had to begin pulling their weight.

Of course, it wasn't as though SMU and Rice were trying to be bad and unpopular. The SWC could have been in 1990, but the smaller schools had been given a short reprieve. They would try, in the meantime, to get better. As a backup plan, though, they would also try to lure others into the fold to do some of their work.

Even after the Big East gobbled its way to eight football teams, fourteen schools continued to play football as independents in 1992 (not counting Penn State, which technically joined the Big Ten for the 1993 season). Most of these remaining independent programs would do no good for the SWC, either because of geography, lack of quality, or both. A few were unattainable; Notre Dame, for example, certainly wasn't coming to the SWC. Louisville and Southern Mississippi were right in the sweet spot of quality and geographic convenience, and convincing those two schools to join might provide just enough stability to prop up the conference. But neither team was budging. Despite having been left out of the other conferences, and despite facing all of the challenges endemic to being an independent program, neither school was interested in hitching themselves to the faltering SWC.

Exciting, briefly, was the possibility the SWC might procure a more valuable prize. Former Oklahoma head coach Barry Switzer campaigned throughout the early 1990s for the Sooners to join their rivals to the south. Cooler, wiser heads in the Oklahoma administration resisted the calls, and the episode stopped before ever really starting.

While the small teams were attempting to make the SWC look as appealing and steady as possible, the larger schools perched themselves near the exits. Texas investigated the hole in the Big Ten's membership, but geography proved too big of a concern for both sides, and the proceedings never made it past the investigation stage. As Texas looked north, Texas A&M looked east towards the SEC. But with twelve teams and no decent options for team number fourteen, interest from the SEC in the Aggies was lukewarm.

The SWC puttered along until 1994. That year, the SEC accepted its national television contract with CBS, the revenue for which the SEC would be keeping entirely for itself. Any sense of camaraderie between the conferences which had battled the NCAA for television rights was now gone. The CFA was dead. Without the CFA's protection, the SWC would need to go alone to the television networks for its next deal. The response by the networks was likely to be pathetic. Any escape by Texas and Texas A&M needed to be made before the next round of negotiations.

Immediately north, the Big Eight had much the same problems as the SWC, though much less severely. Like the SEC, the Big Eight depended more upon the vigor of its fans than the control of large television markets. The few states that the Big Eight encompassed—Iowa, Nebraska, Kansas, Oklahoma, and Colorado—were mostly rural and depopulated, with only a handful of sizeable urban areas between endless fields of corn.

But the Big Eight, unlike the SWC, was not a toxic brand, and its small size allowed for easy expansion, especially now that the SEC had set the precedent for twelve-team conferences. The SWC, despite its compactness, did carry several markets of significance; Dallas and Houston would become, by far, the largest television markets in the Big Eight should the Texas schools join. Great Plains schools could use annual trips into the Lone Star State as a recruiting advantage, hopefully convincing a few Texas high school athletes to come north each season.

Like the SEC, the Big Eight now had to decide who and how many teams should be included. A wholesale merger of the SWC and Big Eight would be counterproductive; SMU, TCU, and Rice were drains on a conference's resources regardless of whether that conference had eight or sixteen teams. And in any event, the sixteen-team experiment was still unproven.

Texas and Texas A&M would be obvious additions, if those schools were willing to accept the invitation. Past that point, opinions within the Big Eight differed, with some voices calling for further expansion into the Rocky Mountain area (BYU, Utah, and, peculiarly, New Mexico were considered the main potential targets in this region). Others within the Big Eight were satisfied with ten teams, which wouldn't get the Big Eight a championship game, but would avoid expansion merely for expansion's sake.

Their decision would largely be made for it. Both of the big Texas programs were state schools; the Texas legislature, in large part, controlled the purse strings for the two. Should the big programs depart to the Big Eight, there wouldn't be enough duct tape in Texas to hold the SWC together as a major conference. The six other SWC schools would be out in the cold unless some other conference came to save them.

Observers still disagree about the amount of pressure Texas politicians put upon the two major programs to play nice with their little brothers. Here is what we know: Pete Laney, the Speaker of the Texas House of Representatives, was a graduate of Texas Tech University. Texas governor Ann Richards was a graduate of Baylor. No high-ranking Texas state politician in 1994 was a graduate of Rice, TCU, SMU, or Houston. Neither Texas Tech nor Baylor was an *outlandish* option for the Big Eight, as SMU, for example, would have been. Lubbock may be in the middle of nowhere, but in a way, that was a good thing; Texas Tech at least was not yet another school clustered between Dallas and Houston. Plus, the Red Raiders had been pretty good—only one season under .500 in the SWC since 1986. The case for Baylor was a bit tougher to make. For one thing, Baylor *was* yet another school wedged between Dallas and Houston, and it was not as though the Waco television market was much of a prize. For decades, Baylor was one of the programs at the very bottom of the conference, although they had enjoyed a slight uptick over the past half-decade. Whether or not pressure on Texas and Texas A&M by politicians saved Baylor and Texas Tech, it is doubtlessly true that pressure by Texas and Texas A&M saved the two other schools. The major programs made clear that they would remain in the SWC without inclusion of Texas Tech and Baylor in any Big Eight expansion. Perhaps it was a bluff. But if it was, it was never called.

The new conference—the Big 12—was fashioned as a merger, not an expansion of the Big Eight. That is, the SWC and Big Eight ceased to exist, with the new twelve-team entity wiping away the old conferences. This merger was mere face-saving for the Texas schools. The SWC, not the Big Eight, was in danger of losing major-conference status. The SWC, not the Big Eight, would be shedding teams to adapt to the new structure. And while the SWC teams—even at the top—were struggling to maintain relevance nationally, the Big Eight could boast multiple legitimate national championship contenders.

For the bottom half of the SWC, the end had finally come. Rice, TCU, SMU, and Houston would be the first teams since Idaho and Montana in the 1950s to be involuntarily removed from a major conference. Where every other program in the nation was doing everything it could to join a conference, the SWC quartet had independence thrust upon them.

***

Their stint in the independence wilderness would not last long—not even a game, as things turned out. A bad conference was better than no conference at all, and the programs left out by the major conferences bonded to form their own associations. The WAC—the king of the minor conferences—added three of the four shunned SWC teams, plus several other schools. By 1996, the WAC had swollen to sixteen teams, the first conference to test the superconference hypothesis.

The WAC's experiment was a failure. With the conference stretching from Honolulu to Tulsa, travel costs skyrocketed. Because eight-team divisions would have left little occasion for the teams in the two divisions to play one another, the WAC split into four quadrants, with each quadrant having four teams. In splitting up the quadrants, however, the WAC destroyed several old rivalries and angered old members. After three years, half of the WAC split away to create the Mountain West Conference ("MWC"). Like the Southern Conference a half-century before, the WAC could not sustain so large a membership.

While the WAC and MWC corralled the underclass of the Pacific coast and Rockies, Conference USA provided a home to the other half of the country's minor programs. Originally a basketball-only conference, Conference USA added football in

1996. In essence, Conference USA became what the Metro Conference would have been had the Metro Conference adopted football after the departures of Florida State and South Carolina.

Only eight teams remained independent by 1998. Of the eight, five were unwanted by even the smallest conferences; eventually, three of the five would join the bottom-of-the-barrel Sun Belt Conference, one would join the WAC, and another would join Conference USA. Of the other three independent schools, the University of Central Florida ("UCF") was relatively young, having established its football program only in 1979 and moved up to Division I-A only in 1996. With its location in Orlando and large student base, UCF would not remain independent for long, and soon UCF also joined Conference USA. The seventh independent program was Navy, a service academy with unique cultural reasons for wanting to remain apart from the conferences.

***

The eighth independent program was Notre Dame. While every other school in the nation was relinquishing independence, or seeking to avoid it, Notre Dame embraced their freedom from the conference structure. NBC's national television contract—the first national television contract for an individual program since Penn's 1950 deal with ABC—made that embrace easy, since the Fighting Irish did not have to split their television money with anyone else. Bowl revenue was always uncertain, since there was no guarantee that Notre Dame would stay at the top of the pyramid. Still, the Irish had been near the peak of the college football world for so long that it could afford to take their chances without a conference.

But Notre Dame could only make that gamble if the bowls remained available to them. Notre Dame helped found the Bowl Coalition, and made Bowl Coalition games all three years of its existence, but future iterations of college football's "playoffs" might not be so forgiving to independents. The 1995 move towards the Bowl Alliance reduced the number of openings from twelve to six, and only two (at most) of those openings could be earned by independent schools. Next time the Bowl Alliance evolved, the conferences might shut independents out entirely.

The two sides disagree as to which party placed the first call, but by 1994, the Big Ten and Notre Dame were in communication with one another. After expanding to include Penn State, the Big Ten had eleven teams, one fewer than required to stage a conference championship game. Since that time, the SEC expanded to twelve teams, the Big East began playing football (and took eight independent teams off the market), the ACC grabbed another valuable program in Florida State, and the SWC was nearing completion of its merger with the Big Eight. Big Ten leaders had said that they were satisfied with eleven teams, but few believed them. Such a strange number, eleven: odd, prime, polysyllabic. The conference would no doubt target another.

Notre Dame—the biggest independent prize in the nation— would be the obvious choice, it was thought, if the Big Ten could have them. But there were concerns within the Big Ten about the Irish, including many of the same concerns that Fielding Yost had voiced almost a century before. The Catholic school was, in many ways, not a good "cultural" fit, with this time religion being less the concern than academics. Big Ten presidents unanimously supported Penn State's entry to the conference because of the school's strong graduate research programs. Notre Dame, on the other hand, was very much an undergraduate institution; in fact, it prided itself on as much. Should Notre Dame be admitted to the CIC, it could never hope to contribute as much as it took from the rest of the members in research money. Still, the Big Ten— prodded this time by the athletic departments, not the presidents—moved ahead. As did the athletic conference at Notre Dame; the fears about being the only independent of consequence remaining on the map sufficiently frightened the Irish towards action.

Given the number of disagreements the two sides had, it is slightly amazing that conversations advanced past even the most preliminary of discussions. The Big Ten insisted upon an even distribution of television revenue; Notre Dame hoped to retain the NBC contract, and the money therefrom, for itself. The Big Ten insisted that Notre Dame play an eight-game conference schedule, just as everyone else did; Notre Dame pointed to rivalries against USC, Boston College, and Navy as reasons that the Big Ten should permit the school greater flexibility in scheduling. The Big Ten wanted Notre Dame to participate in the CIC in only a limited capacity; here, reversing their stance on football television revenue, Notre Dame wanted full participation (and full distribution of grant money) within the CIC.

As these talks continued, the Big East Conference seized its opportunity. If the Irish were unwilling to tether themselves to the lucrative Big Ten, they would be far less likely to join the Big East for football. But what about for all the other sports? If Notre Dame joined the Big East as a non-football member, the Irish could retain their NBC television contract and play whomever they wanted each season, all while securing a home for the two dozen or so sports for which independence was neither lucrative nor convenient.

Like Miami before, Notre Dame was not much of a basketball power, so its inclusion would frustrate at least a couple of the basketball-only members in the Big East. More immediately worrisome for the Big East, however, was that several of its football-only members resented having been kept at arm's length from the rest of the conference. This was fine while those programs had stable conferences in which to send their secondary teams, but as those minor conferences suffered the effects of expansion, the football-only teams complained that their basketball programs should be afforded the same respect as, say, Florida State's moribund basketball program when it joined the hardwood-centric ACC. And certainly, should the Big East grant an invitation to Notre Dame for *basketball*, it should extend the same courtesy to the teams that saved the conference from destruction in 1990.

Struggling to accommodate the various factions within the conference, the Big East bought off the complainers. Notre Dame was extended an invitation to play basketball. So too would Rutgers and West Virginia, thus making six "full" Big East members, seven basketball-only members, and only two football-only members. For Notre Dame, the arrangement was convenient, but nothing more. The Big East, of course, hoped that marriage of convenience might someday develop into true love, and that when the time inevitably came for Notre Dame to join a conference, it would look to the partner closest at hand.

Five years passed before the Notre Dame issue reignited. During that time, Notre Dame's stature had slipped, albeit slightly. Appearances in Bowl Alliance/BCS bowls had become rarer; Notre Dame missed the postseason entirely following the 1996 season, and settled for middling bowl appearances in 1997 and 1998. Those misses meant millions of dollars lost for the university, which did not have to split bowl revenue but, by the same token, had no partners with which to share in bowl proceeds. The wheel was turning, as all independent programs had feared would someday happen to them, and while 100 percent ownership of football revenue was a blessing in boom years, it would be a curse when success vanished.

So again in 1999, talks began between the Big Ten and Notre Dame. The issues that had scuttled the 1994 talks never disappeared, however, and the interminable haggling over details exhausted both sides. Academics at Notre Dame mostly supported the move—the Notre Dame Faculty Senate voted 25–4 in favor of joining the CIC (and thus the Big Ten)—though prominent academics within the school spoke out against the move towards graduate research at the expense of undergraduate instruction. And although there was still resistance at a few Big Ten schools, and many details still to be worked out between the sides, the conference was ready to accept Notre Dame as its twelfth team.

This time, however, the Catholics successfully raised the "culture" complaints. "Does this core identity of Notre Dame as Catholic, private and independent," asked university president Edward Malloy, "seem a match for an association of universities— even a splendid association of great universities—that are uniformly secular, predominantly state institutions and with a long heritage of conference affiliation?"

"Our answer to that question, in the final analysis, is no."

After a century of charting its own course, too many people within Notre Dame's community opposed a redefinition of their institution. Students and fans chanted "No Big Ten" at campus basketball games during the 1999 negotiations. Signs with anti-Big Ten slogans appeared in dormitory windows. A dedicated rump faction of professors—one must assume a minority from the Faculty Senate vote, though it is impossible to know for sure— publicly spoke out against the move. Despite the enthusiasm shown, at least at times, by both the athletic department and the faculty for a move, the Notre Dame Board of Trustees voted 39–0 in February 1999 against joining the Big Ten.

The unanimity of the decision may not have truly represented opinion on campus, but it did send a message to every conference. Independence was no longer simply a state of being; it was, for Notre Dame, an end in and of itself. If the CIC—and millions of dollars in research money every year—could not convince Notre Dame to join the Big Ten, no conference would be able to change their minds. By 2012, Notre Dame would be one of two teams (along with Navy) to have never belonged to a football conference. As of this writing, Navy is scheduled to abandon independence in 2015.

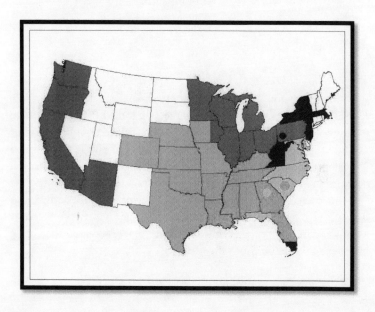

The college football world in 1996. The Pac-10 remains the same, but the Big Eight and SWC have now merged to create the Big 12. The Big Ten has expanded to include Penn State, while the ACC now includes Florida State, and the SEC stretches to Arkansas and South Carolina. In addition, the Big East has become a full conference, playing football along with basketball and non-revenue sports. While only Iowa had teams in two major conferences in 1977, six states now have teams in multiple major conferences, with teams from three major conferences in Florida. Splits within states are meant to reflect only geography, not relative popularity.

Every major American team sport—except college football, that is—ends its season with a playoff. In the NFL, the playoff is a single-elimination tournament: a team is out of the playoffs after one loss. College basketball follows a similar single-elimination system, with most conferences using single-elimination tournaments of their own to determine which teams get into the main NCAA "March Madness" tournament. The NBA, MLB, and the NHL, on the other hand, use multi-game series instead of single-elimination games for their playoffs, but the basic tournament structure is the same.

So pervasive is the playoff in American sports that many non-team sports have grafted postseasons onto their schedules, no matter how awkward the fit might be. NASCAR, for example, has the Sprint Cup Series, a set of ten races at the end of the season that determine stock car racing's champion. Qualification for the Series depends upon performance in the earlier "regular season" races. Similarly, the Professional Golf Association ("PGA") permits into the PGA Championship only those golfers who meet certain performance goals in previous tournaments. Horse racing has the Breeders' Cup, a set of invitation-only races for top thoroughbreds.

Then there is college football, the lone oddball, as is so often the case. Michigan's 1902 Rose Bowl victory predates even the World Series, so in some ways college football pioneered the use of a postseason in American sports. But until the 1960s, the Associated Press awarded its championship before the bowl games were played; the college football postseason had no effect on which team was named champion. A two-team "playoff" was not introduced until 1992, and until 1998, there was no guarantee this tournament of sorts would even occur. Even with the introduction of a four-team playoff—scheduled to begin after the 2014 season—the scope of the new college football playoff (4 of 124 teams) differs considerably from that of the NFL (12 of 32 teams), MLB (10 of 30 teams), the NBA (16 of 30 teams), or the NHL (again 16 of 30 teams).

Such drastic anomalies cannot go uncriticized. Those anomalies also cannot survive without supporters. Both sides of the college football playoff argument are guilty of empty sloganeering. Playoff opponents argue that restricted postseasons make every regular season "count," but of course that isn't true. College football teams have gone undefeated and not made the championship game, meaning none of those teams' games "counted" for championship purposes. Plus, with a small postseason, teams are more quickly eliminated from contention: lose once and their championship hopes are in critical condition; lose twice and they are almost assuredly dead. The games following each team's second loss thus count for very little, at least as far as the national championship is concerned.

On the other hand, proponents of larger playoffs argue that teams should have a chance to "prove on the field" which squad is the best. But isn't that what teams are supposed to be doing during the regular season—proving "on the field" that they are the best in the league? With a small (or no) playoff, the proving comes in September through December instead of January.

Every system for determining a champion faces irresolvable tradeoffs. All things being equal, each regular-season loss is more important in leagues with smaller postseasons. To take an extreme example, if every team makes the postseason, regular-season losses matter little, since every team can still win the final tournament. Over half of the NHL's teams make the playoffs; the 2012 Los Angeles Kings won the Stanley Cup despite *losing* more games than they won during the regular season.

A downside to smaller postseasons, however, is that many strong teams are eliminated from championship contention early in the year. If there is no playoff at all, each regular season loss is crippling. From 1950 to 1991 (when the Bowl Coalition was created), only once did the Associated Press national champion lose two games. Fewer fans will continue watching after their team's first loss if they know that, no matter what happens during the rest of the season, their team has little chance to win the championship. And leagues with no postseason miss out on the excitement that high-stakes playoff games generate.

Once you understand the tradeoffs, the playoffs-versus-no-playoffs preference is—for fans—simply a matter of taste, no different than Pepsi versus Coke. If you enjoy elimination games throughout the season and don't like the eighth-best or sixteenth-best team during the regular season winning a championship, you prefer smaller playoffs. If you enjoy high-pressure games at the end of the year and Cinderella-style upsets, you prefer bigger playoffs.

***

Professional sports leagues, contrary to belief, are not set up to determine the best team. They are set up, like any other business, to make money. It makes no difference to the leagues whether 5 percent or 95 percent of the revenue comes from the regular season, as long as the total figure is as great as possible. If, say, Congress passed a law saying that professional football postseason revenue will henceforth be taxed at 100 percent, the NFL would do everything possible to diminish the value of its postseason and enhance the importance of its regular season.

College football's divide was not quite as stark as the 100-percent-tax hypothetical example, but the same principles applied. Because the NCAA controlled the regular-season television contract, schools looked for alternative ways to earn revenue without having to split the money with smaller programs through the NCAA. A full playoff wasn't a solution—the NCAA controlled tournaments, too—but the bowl games were a loophole grandfathered into the system from before anyone contemplated television contracts. Because teams and conferences kept bowl revenue for themselves, they had no interest in changing the bowl system, peculiar though it was.

If the conferences could fashion a more valuable postseason out of the bowls, however, they would control the rights to that revenue. Antitrust law, that pesky hindrance, prevented conferences from entirely shutting out minor programs from a new postseason. Any tournament would have to remain open to all, at least technically. But every spot in the tournament taken up by a minor program was a slice of revenue lost. For the major conferences, the best playoff would enhance the value of the regular season while remaining small enough to fit into their pocket.

The first tentative steps towards such a playoff were taken in 1992, when five of the major conferences—the SEC, ACC, Big East, SWC, and Big Eight—established the Bowl Coalition.

As things stood before 1992, the conferences could not guarantee a final championship game to the television networks. Such a pledge would have been quite valuable. The NFL's Super Bowl was one of the most-watched television programs every year, and while a college championship would never be so popular, networks would pay handsomely for a final championship matchup with anything close to the Super Bowl's ratings. As things stood, the networks could only hope that the bowls happened to provide such a game.

Under the new Bowl Coalition, whenever the #1 and #2 teams came from one of the five participating conferences, those two teams would be matched in a *de facto* championship game. Sometimes this already happened, even without the Coalition. When Nebraska (Big Eight) and Miami (then independent) finished the 1983 season #1 and #2, Nebraska took the Orange

Bowl berth traditionally awarded to the Big Eight champion, and the Orange Bowl then invited Miami to play in what would become the championship game for that season. Other years, the Sugar Bowl or Rose Bowl might become the championship game by similar luck.

But often, the bowl system could not match #1 with #2—like, for example, if the Orange Bowl-bound Big Eight champion and Sugar Bowl-bound SEC champion were #1 and #2. Under the Bowl Coalition, one of those bowls would step aside and allow their top-two team to play in the other bowl, thus creating a championship game.

Unfortunately, the Bowl Coalition never worked as intended. In 1992 and 1993, a "national championship game" between #1 and #2 would have occurred under the old system anyway. In those two years, the Coalition was like an insurance policy that remains unneeded because disaster never comes to pass. If the insurance policy is free, there is no harm in having some extra protection.

Far worse than the irrelevant years was the very real possibility the Bowl Coalition might still fail to produce a championship game. The Big Ten and Pac-10 did not join the Coalition. Those two conferences had played in the Rose Bowl every year since 1947, and their connection to the game extended as far back as 1902, when Fielding Yost's point-a-minute Michigan team defeated Stanford. Over the ensuing century, the Rose Bowl became the Granddaddy of Them All, the reason why New Year's Day is associated with the college football. The Big Ten and Pac-10 owned equity in the most valuable property in college football, and neither conference was willing to give up that space, even if it meant that their schools would forgo a chance to win the national championship.

There also remained a cultural divide between the Rose Bowl conferences and the others. Recall that the Bowl Coalition conferences were also the conferences of the College Football

Association, with the WAC replaced by the Big East (most Big East programs had belonged to the CFA as independents). The Pac-10 and Big Ten resisted the television revolution and aligned with the NCAA during the litigation, though they quickly reevaluated the wisdom of their position after the NCAA contract was finally struck down in 1984. Less than a decade had passed since the Supreme Court had settled the television question, and old wounds had not yet healed.

Because the Pac-10 and Big Ten (and the Rose Bowl) did not join the Bowl Coalition, if a team from one of those conferences finished the season #1 or #2, it could not play in the championship game. After the final week of the 1994 regular season, only two teams held perfect records: Penn State of the Big Ten, and Nebraska of the Big Eight. As Big Ten champion, Penn State was obligated to play the Pac-10 champion in the Rose Bowl; matching Penn State with Nebraska was impossible. A loss by either Penn State or Nebraska have answered the national championship question in the other's favor, but Penn State easily handled Oregon 38–20 in the Rose Bowl on New Year's Day, and Nebraska defeated #3 Miami 24–17 the next night in the Orange Bowl.

Directly comparing the two teams was impossible, since they never played one another. Indirectly comparing them was tricky too; Nebraska and Penn State did not share a common opponent during the 1994 season. Debates about which team was better were driven by nothing more than conjecture. Nebraska entered the Orange Bowl ranked #1 by the Associated Press, and voters left that ranking in place after Nebraska's victory over Miami, though ten AP voters dissented and voted Penn State as their top team. The non-unanimous result was unsatisfying, but any result in absence of seeing the teams play one another would have been unsatisfying, both to fans and to television networks.

The Rose Bowl fissure was the Bowl Coalition's most obvious shortcoming, but the Coalition also often failed to arrange compelling games in its lesser bowls. The six 1994–95 Coalition bowl games—that is, the games that were supposed to be at the upper tier of the postseason structure—included 6-5 Texas Tech and 6-4-1 Notre Dame. Both of those teams lost their bowl game by over two touchdowns. Meanwhile, the WAC finished with three teams in the top #25, including #10 Utah, but none were invited to play in Coalition bowls.

Inflexibility—both in the championship game and outside of it—doomed the Coalition. Twelve teams were needed to fill the Coalition bowl games. The Bowl Coalition guaranteed slots to two teams apiece from the Big East, Big Eight, SEC, ACC, and SWC, regardless of how worthy those conferences and teams may have been. If 6-5 Texas Tech were from any other conference, it would have been left out of the postseason entirely. But because Texas Tech played in the weakened and scandal-plagued SWC, it was launched into a premier game against competition it had no business playing. Similarly, because Notre Dame had a special seat at the table due to its continued success as the last remaining substantial independent program, it played in a top bowl each of the three seasons the Bowl Coalition was in place, even when—as in 1994—it did not deserve to do so. This left only one at-large spot for the rest of the nation, regardless of how good those other teams might have been (or how bad the major-conference teams were).

The conferences and bowls reworked the system in 1995, with the Bowl Alliance replacing the Bowl Coalition. Six bowls were reduced to three: the Fiesta, Sugar, and Orange bowls. The Bowl Alliance no longer guaranteed spots to the runners-up of conferences; only conference champions earned automatic entry into the Alliance bowls. Quality of competition thus improved, as did flexibility. Although the Big Ten remained apart from the Bowl Coalition, that conference allowed its teams to accept bids to Bowl Alliance games, as long as the Big Ten champion still played in the Rose Bowl. This opened another pool of quality teams to the Alliance's potential invite list, resulting in more attractive games and thus more money.

Still, the largest problem endured. The Big Ten and Pac-10 remained contractually obligated to the Rose Bowl, which in turn was obligated to ABC. Rose Bowl executives feared that allowing one of the two conference champions to abandon their game for a national championship contest elsewhere—at precisely the moment when those teams, with a top-two national ranking, were most valuable—would invalidate the Rose Bowl's television contract. The conferences, in turn, feared that joining the Alliance would break their contract with the Rose Bowl, permanently damaging their reputation with the most valuable game in college sports.

Integration was inevitable, however. Too many parties, including the conferences and the Rose Bowl itself, wanted a piece of the championship game action. The initial Bowl Alliance contract was set at three years, running through the 1997 football season. The Rose Bowl's television contract, not coincidentally, also expired after the 1997 season. By June 1996, a reasonable compromise had been reached. The Rose Bowl would become the fourth Bowl Alliance game in 1998. The championship game would rotate between the Rose, Sugar, Fiesta, and Orange Bowls, each receiving the game once every four years. The Rose Bowl would keep its traditional New Year's Day afternoon time slot during those years in which it was not the national championship game. Finally, the Big Ten and Pac-10 champions were guaranteed a spot in the Rose Bowl, unless one of those teams were ranked #1 or #2 and sent instead to the national championship game. Thus the Bowl Championship Series ("BCS") was born.

***

The BCS was delightfully simple and fiendishly complex. Like the Bowl Coalition and Bowl Alliance, the BCS was a playoff of two teams. After the regular season, the top two teams in the country would be sent to the Rose, Sugar, Fiesta, or Orange Bowl, depending upon the year. Teams from all conferences—including the Pac-10 and Big Ten—were now eligible to play in the championship game. The other major-conference champions, along with two at-large teams, would play in the remaining three bowl games.

The tricky part was determining the best two teams in the country. Before the Bowl Coalition, different groups awarded their own national championships; in 1990, for example, the Associated Press awarded Colorado its championship, while United Press International gave its prize to Georgia Tech. The championship game was supposed to overcome this split national championship problem by pairing the two teams most likely to earn such a split championship.

But just as groups of pollsters often disagreed about which team was best, those groups also disagreed about which team should be ranked second, which should be ranked third, and so on. This had once been unimportant, but now the #2 ranking was as significant as #1 at the end of the season, since those two teams received equal spots in the final game.

Instead of choosing one traditional poll to be official, the BCS combined several human polls and computer ratings, averaged the results, and used that amalgamation to produce the official BCS rankings. By including all major parties, the BCS hoped to prevent any arguments the poll voters might later make about awarding their own national championship to a different team.

The BCS's first season, 1998, provides a spectacular example of the potential selection glitches. Tennessee—SEC champions and undefeated during the regular season—was the undisputed #1 team in the country heading into the bowls. But what about #2? Ohio State spent much of the season at #1, winning each of its first eight games by seventeen points or more (including wins over the #7, #8, and #21 teams in the country), but the Buckeyes then lost a home game against unranked Michigan State and finished 10–1. Or how about Wisconsin, which, like Ohio State, played in the Big Ten and finished the regular season 10–1? Maybe Kansas State, which went into the Big 12 Championship Game undefeated but lost to #10 Texas A&M in double overtime by a field goal? How about Pac-10 champion UCLA, which went undefeated until dropping a non-conference game at Miami in December? Or maybe Tulane, the only team besides Tennessee to finish the year undefeated, but which played in the weak Conference USA and did not defeat a ranked team all season? Or perhaps Florida State, which won the ACC, lost only one game, and entered bowl season on a ten-game winning streak, yet lost its starting quarterback— future Heisman Trophy winner Chris Weinke—to injury shortly before the bowls?

Florida State was chosen, though any of those teams would have been reasonable selections. Because Tennessee won the championship game, controversy was postponed; no one argued that the Volunteers were undeserving national champions. But had Florida State won the national championship game, many people would have claimed that Ohio State, or Wisconsin, or even Tulane should have played in the championship game instead, having finished the year with similar records and accomplishments as Florida State.

Selection problems extended beyond the championship game. Six of the eight teams chosen overall for BCS bowls were chosen by an objective metric: conference championships. The other two teams were chosen from the remaining at-large pool, with the bowls using the BCS rankings to select their teams.

But there was no rule that the non-championship BCS bowls had to choose the *highest* ranked teams, only that they not go too far down the list for their at-large selections. Returning to 1998, Kansas State finished the regular season undefeated, lost the Big 12 Championship game to 10–1 Texas A&M in double overtime, and was #3 in the BCS rankings following that loss. Instead of Kansas State, however, the Sugar and Orange Bowls chose lower ranked but more popular Florida and Ohio State, leaving the #3 team in the country entirely outside the major bowls. A "Kansas State Rule" was put into place following 1998 guaranteeing entrance to a BCS bowl for any team finishing the year in the top four, but higher ranked at-large teams could still be, and frequently were, passed over for schools that were more popular.

Another perpetual source of discord was the computer ratings used as part of the official BCS rankings. Computers were supposed to act as a counterweight to the human pollsters, who might exhibit bias or whose groupthink might cause deserving teams to go unnoticed. The computer ratings, generally speaking, also kept small-conference schools from rising too far in the rankings, since teams from those small conferences would not face many quality opponents. When BYU won its national championship in 1984, the New York Times computer poll ranked the Cougars *tenth* in the country. In 1998, undefeated Tulane, already ranked only tenth by human pollsters, was ranked thirteenth by the computer ratings, lower than 8–3 Nebraska.

This computer bias against minor conference teams strengthened when the BCS ordered the programmers to eliminate margin of victory in its ratings, ostensibly for sportsmanship purposes; there were fears that powerful teams would hammer cupcake opponents by eighty points just to get a ratings boost. But taking away margin of victory deprived minor-conference teams of evidence of their quality, at least in the computer equations. BYU or Tulane might defeat Southwest Louisiana by fifty, but all the computer would see is a win over inferior competition, not the dominance of the victory.

Rumblings once again spread of antitrust problems. The big schools, so the argument ran, had formed a cartel through the BCS and monopolized the major bowls. It was a tricky argument to make—the large conferences controlled the bowls well before the BCS, so it was unclear how the BCS placed additional restraints on trade—but interested politicians from states with overlooked schools waived the antitrust banner, just as the CFA had done in the 1980s against the NCAA.

More immediately damaging to the BCS's reputation was its inability to mesh the computer ratings with the human polls. Some seasons, the computer ratings were redundant, since they mostly agreed with what human pollsters were saying. Whenever computer ratings played a decisive role in the selection process, though, people complained. However nice the notion of a bias-free system for selecting teams may have been in the abstract, fans resented that a black box could override the opinion of flesh and blood voters.

In 2003, for example, the computer ratings proved critical. USC, ranked #1 in the human polls, was left out of the championship game because of low computer scores. Theoretically, the computer ratings were in place to do exactly what they did: use objective data to downgrade a team "overrated" by regular pollsters. In reality, fans resented that the championship game would not include the team every major human poll agreed was the best in the nation. The Associated Press, furious that its placement of USC as #1 went ignored, dropped out of the BCS in protest, depriving the system of a source of legitimacy.

These twin attacks—legal rumblings from teams at the bottom, and dissatisfaction from fans that top teams were left out—led to a reworking of the system in 2004. The computer ratings remained part of the system but were significantly neutered, now counting for only one-third of the overall BCS rankings, not half. Moreover, the computer ratings were reengineered to mimic the human voters (which defeated the purpose of having computer ratings in the first place). No team ranked in the top two of the major human polls has been left out of the championship game since 2003.

At the bottom end, lower conferences pushed for a new game to be added to the BCS collection, which would open up four at-large spots instead of two and thus potentially provide more access to those games for minor-conference teams. The BCS obliged, detaching the national championship game from the bowls and thus creating five games—the BCS National Championship game, plus the Rose, Sugar, Fiesta, and Orange Bowls.

The minor conferences also lobbied for safeguards in cases when their members were highly ranked. Fearing antitrust complaints, the BCS again obliged. The highest-ranked winner of a minor conference was provided an automatic berth in the BCS if that team were ranked #12 or higher. From 1998 through 2003, no teams from minor conferences attended BCS bowl games. Seven have done so since.

***

All that is a quick history of a process that never stopped evolving, as almost no one stopped complaining at any point about some injustice or another, real or perceived, perpetrated by the BCS.

The BCS had been designed to comport with college football's power structure. After the disbandment of the SWC and the transformation of the Big East into a football conference, six conferences—the ACC, Big East, Big Ten, Big 12, Pac-10, and SEC—possessed teams that, any given year, might be good enough to be called national champion. The programs within those conferences were, with only a few exceptions, the most powerful in the nation. During the first few years of the BCS's existence, there was a clear division between the weakest major conference and the most powerful "non-BCS" conferences. No other conference had a legitimate gripe—at least based on the quality of their play—that they belonged in the exclusive club.

The relative power of the conferences influenced the BCS structure, but so too did the BCS structure begin affecting the relative power of the conferences. The top six conferences were assured a spot at the table, and their champions would attend one of the major bowl games. Yet there was no guarantee that six would forever remain the correct number, or that the half-dozen conferences on top in 2003 would remain dominant. Inclusion in the Bowl Coalition failed to save the SWC from being torn apart by its rivals, and the BCS might prove no better a shield for its participants.

***

Mike Tranghese, commissioner of the Big East, understood the precarious position his hybrid conference occupied. To the west stood the Big Ten, stuck awkwardly at eleven teams. The twelfth Big Ten member—and no doubt there would be a twelfth Big Ten member eventually—would probably come from the east; its newest member, Penn State, came from the Mid-Atlantic region, and a return to that area seemed likely. Tranghese's fledgling football conference was in danger of destruction at the hands of the century-old bully next door. Should the Big Ten extend an offer to, say, Syracuse, conference loyalty would likely count for little against the monetary boon the Big Ten could offer.

Unlike the other major conferences, the Big East's membership included schools that did not play Division I-A college football. Until 1991, the Big East was not a football conference at all. The conference made a go of things on the football side after it persuaded Miami, one of the most valuable prizes available during the land grab of independent schools, to join. In so doing, the Big East saved itself, while similar non-football arrangements, such as the Metro Conference, crumbled.

By 1998, the Big East had enjoyed seven seasons playing football. It was one of the six major conferences whose champions were automatically invited to participate in BCS bowls. The Big East had convinced Notre Dame to join—at least for basketball and non-revenue sports—over entreaties by the Big Ten. Three of the conference's eight football teams would finish the 1998 season ranked in the top 25. Five Big East teams would make the men's basketball tournament that season, tied for most of any conference that year.

Just as in 1990, however, football threatened to undercut the Big East's success. And just as in 1990, the unbridgeable divide between the conference's full members and basketball-only members almost proved the conference's undoing.

Fifteen teams boasted Big East affiliation in 1998. Two—Virginia Tech and Temple—belonged to the conference only for football (Virginia Tech would begin playing basketball in the Big East in 1999). Seven—Notre Dame, Connecticut, St. John's, Providence, Georgetown, Villanova, and Seton Hall—belonged to the Big East only for basketball and non-revenue sports. All of the basketball-only schools except Notre Dame lacked Division I-A football teams, though Connecticut was moving towards that at the time. The final six programs—Boston College, Pittsburgh, Syracuse, Miami, Rutgers, and West Virginia—played all sports, including football, in the Big East.

These multiple levels of membership were a never-ending source of friction. The basketball-only programs opposed further expansion, since the thirteen-team basketball league was already quite diluted compared to the dominating nine-team conference of the 1980s. With only eight teams, however, the Big East *football* conference was smaller than any other major conference in the country, and it could only get to eight by including perpetual losers Temple and Rutgers. None of the basketball-only schools were suitable additions for football except Notre Dame, and the Irish weren't joining the football conference any time soon.

One of the Big East's factions would have to stand down. The football programs argued that without further expansion by the conference, the football schools would be placed at such an economic disadvantage that continuing association in the Big East would be impossible. The basketball programs countered that more expansion was untenable, since further watering down the Big East's basketball product would threaten to make those programs irrelevant nationally. Only one side could get their way.

Money heals all wounds. Had the post-football Big East been a financial success, the factions may have been able to paper over their squabbles with cash. But the economic windfall that was supposed to result from a conference encompassing all of America's major eastern urban centers failed to materialize. For all its population—and even though the area Northeast was the cradle of college football—New England today has fewer college football fans per capita than any other region in the country, and the new look Big East failed to change that reality. Population counts for little if no one is watching your games.

Commissioner Tranghese represented all factions of the Big East, even though the interests of the two sides were incompatible. His heart, however, was with basketball. Tranghese accepted expansion into football in 1990 only at last resort, and he regarded the Big East's move as the source of the conference's continuing weakness. Had the Big East never expanded, Tranghese believed, the conference would still be the cohesive nine-team unit that dominated college basketball in the 1980s and earned plenty of money for everyone in the process.

Rather than search for perhaps non-existent common ground between the factions, Tranghese offered a sacrifice to his neighbors. Under Tranghese's proposal, the Big East would unilaterally abandon football, "merging" with the ACC by sending Miami, Pitt, and Syracuse to that conference for football only. If the ACC were to accept the offer, the Big East would remain a preeminent basketball conference, thus protecting its non-football members, and there would be very little left for any other rivals to poach. Life would return to that halcyon pre-expansion era. And if Virginia Tech or West Virginia wanted thereafter to leave the Big East in order to save their football programs, so be it; the basketball conference would be that much stronger because of it.

The ACC demurred. Football-only membership was one reason the Big East lacked cohesion, and the ACC was uninterested in adopting that dysfunctional system. The two conferences dropped the matter after a few short discussions, and the Big East's internecine basketball-football feud continued.

***

Despite rejecting Tranghese's sacrificial offer, ACC leadership rather liked the idea of stealing a few of the Big East's more valuable football programs, as long as the stealing took place on the ACC's terms.

Like the Big East, the ACC had long been considered a basketball conference first and foremost, though unlike the Big East, all ACC programs throughout the conference's history played Division I-A football. The ACC's nucleus was in North Carolina, where the four Tobacco Road schools of Duke, Wake Forest, North Carolina, and North Carolina State fell within a narrow band along Interstate 40. All four schools were known primarily for their basketball prowess, and none of the four represented the conference particularly well in football.

That perception of the ACC changed, at least a bit, with the addition of Florida State in 1991. The Seminoles finished every season from 1987 to 2000 in the top five of the Associated Press poll, including national championships in 1993 and 1999. With Florida State, the ACC possessed a consistent, powerful representative during BCS bowl play and a national championship contender every season.

Unfortunately, only Florida State provided the ACC with those things. The Seminoles won a share of every ACC championship from 1992, its first season in the conference, until 2000, plus championships in 2002 and 2003. Florida State moved to the ACC, at least in part, to take advantage of that lack of parity. By joining the ACC, Florida State insured itself a gentle path to the conference championship and major bowl appearances every year.

Such an arrangement—legitimacy, but no parity—was perfect for the ACC of 1991, whose status as a major conference was questionable and often questioned. Florida State provided legitimacy, though at the expense of competitive play. The trade was worth making, since without the Seminoles' involvement, the ACC might be in the same weak position as the Big East, or worse.

Unlike the Big East, whose dual membership structure hampered attempts at expansion and undermined stability as it did expand, the nine-team ACC had plenty of room to accommodate new programs. And although the Seminoles running roughshod over everyone else might have appealed to the otherwise desperate ACC of 1991, the ACC of 2003 did not have to settle.

The conference's first target—its second, third, fourth, and fifth targets too, for the matter—was the University of Miami. As with Florida State and the ACC, Miami's move to the Big East in 1990 provided its new conference with a legitimacy in football that it otherwise would never have acquired. Miami had the pick of any conference in the country from which to choose. But rather than joining the financially stable SEC, Miami—like rival Florida State—chose the path to on-field dominance, accepting an offer from the Big East and helping the conference transition away from its purely basketball foundations.

Miami was no less valuable in 2003 than 1991. As recently as 2001, the Hurricanes won the national championship, and they reappeared in the 2002 national championship game. During this period, the Hurricanes were cultivating more talent than perhaps any team in college football history; beginning in December 2002, players from Miami would score a touchdown in the NFL every week until November 2011.

Miami was an obvious target for the ACC, but teams eleven and twelve would be trickier. The closest Big East football teams geographically, West Virginia and Virginia Tech, were economically unappealing. Although both programs were strong on the field, neither was dominant like Miami. Moreover, those schools' proximity to the ACC hindered their cause. Back in the 1970s, when the Pac-8 was adding two Arizona schools and the SWC was adding Houston to an already Texas-heavy conference, West Virginia or Virginia Tech would have made perfect sense. Travel would be easy, and the new programs could smoothly form new rivalries with other members. But in 2003, television contracts drove expansion decisions. Neither the Charleston nor Morgantown television markets were much of a prize. And both West Virginia and Virginia Tech sat in areas that were already watching ACC games.

Better prospects lay further north, near the Big East's heart. These programs—Syracuse, Pittsburgh, and Boston College in particular—were the schools Mike Tranghese most feared losing when he offered Big East football to the ACC in 1998. Two of the three teams had been founding members of the Big East in 1979, and Pittsburgh joined only a few years later. Syracuse and Pittsburgh were basketball lynchpins, and Boston College was an entryway to the second-largest television market in the Northeast.

The ACC's priority—landing Miami—also influenced its decision to focus on Northeastern teams for the final spots. Despite its location at the southernmost tip of Florida, a large percentage of Miami's alumni base lived in the New England and Mid-Atlantic regions. Adding Northeastern schools might act as an additional enticement for the Hurricanes to enter the fold.

Thus it was settled. Along with Miami, the ACC would chase Syracuse, the strongest football program in New York, and Boston College, the most popular football program in New England.

***

There was only one problem: no one knew whether any of those schools wanted to switch sides. The Big East was young enough that many of its founding fathers were still on the scene. Those men who were present at the Big East's creation were not anxious to see their baby destroyed by a foreign conference, even if the result was a marginally better economic situation for their schools.

Foremost among the Big East's founders was Syracuse men's basketball coach Jim Boeheim. The native of Lyons, New York—located midway between Rochester and Syracuse along Interstate 90—played basketball for the Orange in the mid-1960s, manning a backcourt alongside future Hall of Fame member (and current Detroit mayor) Dave Bing. Boeheim joined the Syracuse coaching staff in 1969, and he took over the program in 1976 at just 32 years old. Although Syracuse straddled the Big East divide between the football programs and basketball programs, there was no doubt that Boeheim's side predominated. For example, the football and basketball teams occupied the same building, the Carrier Dome: the largest college basketball facility in the country, and one of the smallest BCS-conference football facilities.

The original Big East was a Northeastern institution through and through, stretching only as far inland as Pittsburgh and located (except for Georgetown) entirely in states north of the Mason-Dixon line. To Boeheim and the other basketball leaders of the Big East, the 1991 expansion south and into football was, at best, a necessary evil for preserving one of the greatest basketball conferences ever assembled. Paris was worth a mass; Pittsburgh and Boston College were worth bringing Miami into the fold.

Syracuse supported the Big East's move into football, but only because it was necessary for the basketball conference. Leaving the Big East for the ACC, no matter how much financial sense it might have made for Syracuse, would destroy Boeheim's basketball conference. And even if it didn't—even if the Big East somehow survived—Boeheim and Syracuse would no longer be around to participate.

"It's about money, power and football in any order. It's football. It's always football," Boeheim fumed, accurately assessing the situation. The decision, however, ultimately was not his—the ACC and Syracuse's athletic director would have the final say. But could Syracuse really go against the wishes of its patron saint?

***

Meanwhile, resistance to expansion mounted on the opposite side of the table as well. The ACC membership was unanimous in voting to explore possible expansion in March 2003. But by May, that unanimity had broken down.

A few schools—Florida State, Clemson, Maryland, Georgia Tech—were fully supportive of ACC expansion. Three more football teams meant a conference championship game, with the revenue from that game flowing throughout the conference. Furthermore, if Miami were one of those three teams, chances were quite good that the ACC could get multiple teams into BCS bowls every year, meaning even larger payouts for everyone. North Carolina State and Wake Forest were slightly more hesitant about expansion than the above group, but both were generally amenable to the idea if certain academic and travel concerns were addressed.

At the other end of the spectrum were Duke and North Carolina. Opposition at those schools came on two fronts. First, though football concerns drove expansion decisions, Duke and North Carolina's basketball programs were the primary focus of their athletic departments. Adding Miami and Boston College would undercut the ACC's competitive advantage in basketball. If the ACC were to deemphasize basketball, Duke and North Carolina could not fall back upon their moribund football programs. As Mike Krzyzewski, men's basketball coach and Boeheim-like figure at Duke, put it, "Is the football championship that important that it dilutes something else that you have?" At Florida State or Clemson, the answer was a simple yes.

Second, academic leaders at Duke and North Carolina protested against expansion. One fear was that Miami and Boston were too far away. Travel might matter little to the athletic departments, but professors worried that the increased geographic scope of the ACC would be used as an excuse, as one professor carped, "for more free days for students to miss class." Duke President Nan Keohane and North Carolina President James Moeser also voiced disapproval over the quickness with which the ACC had conducted the expansion process. In a little over two months, the ACC moved from exploration to being prepared to add as many new schools as it had added in the previous fifty years combined.

Then there was Virginia. ACC expansion into the Northeast threatened the survival of the Big East, and with it, the survival of Virginia Tech football. Should the Big East disintegrate, the Hokies might end up somewhere safe; then again, they might also be hampered by their rural campus and lack of nearby television markets, the reasons ACC was looking to Syracuse and Boston College rather than Virginia Tech in the first place. Virginia governor Mark Warner and several state legislators pressured the University of Virginia to pledge to vote in favor of ACC expansion only on the condition that Virginia Tech be included.

Ordinarily, the remaining conference members might have ignored Virginia's intransience. But seven votes were needed to approve expansion, and both Duke and North Carolina refused to budge from their resistance. With six votes for and two votes against expansion, Virginia held the deciding ballot. Whether a bluff or a legitimate threat, the school of Jefferson warned that it would withhold support for all expansion—Miami included—unless the ACC invited Virginia's fellow Commonwealth school.

Virginia's stance, in turn, dampened the ACC's chances at luring Miami. The financial conditions of the Big East and ACC were not so different that abandoning the former was an obvious decision, especially when the Big East offered Miami $9 million annually to remain in the conference, an amount not far from the $9.7 million ACC teams had each earned during 2003. And Miami had made clear from the beginning that it valued its opportunities to play in front of its alumni bases in the Northeast. Virginia Tech provided no such prospects.

***

In the background of that maneuvering loomed the ever-present specter of litigation.

Conferences are contractual arrangements, with duties running between schools. Exiting a conference breaches the contract. Rather than leaving matters to a court to determine the damages from such a breach, conferences generally decide in advance how much schools will pay to exit. That predetermined fee is supposed to approximate how much the departure hurts the remaining schools.

In 2003 while the storm was brewing, the Big East's exit fee was $1 million. That figure, reasonable as it may have been when it was set, now seemed insufficient to the remaining Big East members, whose athletic programs would be cast to the wind in the event of their conference's disintegration and uncertain to land on fertile ground.

Despite that predetermined damages clause, Richard Blumenthal—then the Connecticut Attorney General, currently a senator from the same state—pursued a hodgepodge of claims on behalf of his state's flagship university. The harm was not in Miami or Boston College potentially leaving the conference, claimed the crusading Blumenthal. Instead, those schools, along with the ACC, had pursued "a back-room conspiracy, born in secret, founded on greed, and carried out through calculated deceit." Because Connecticut, Pittsburgh, and the other remaining Big East football schools had spent millions of dollars on their football programs under the belief that Miami and Boston College would remain in the conference, the departing universities and the ACC should be liable for those expenditures. Blumenthal claimed these damages totaled "hundreds of millions of dollars," and that, in the meantime, a Connecticut court should enjoin Miami and Boston College from leaving.

The lawsuit had its intended effect, at least initially. Duke and North Carolina, already unsure about the wisdom of expansion, were spooked by the prospect of liability. Even if nothing came of the lawsuit, the ACC schools would undoubtedly spend thousands, maybe millions, defending against it. Further, they would be defending in a foreign state, where the Connecticut Attorney General would be arguing to a Connecticut jury that the University of Connecticut had been harmed by schools from outside Connecticut.

Blumenthal's lawsuit would have been scarier still had it been based on legal, rather than political, calculations. Whether his claims had merit or not—and they did not—Connecticut courts were powerless to hear a case involving the ACC, whose organization sat in North Carolina and none of whose members were located in Connecticut. The federal constitution requires, in the interests of fairness, that defendants have minimum contacts with a state in order to be sued there. (Imagine the difficulty of living in New York and finding out that you were sued in California despite never having been to California and never having done business with Californians.) The court found that the ACC lacked these minimum contacts with Connecticut and dismissed the lawsuit (it made no determination towards defendant Miami at that time.)

At this juncture, the proper thing to do would have been to bring the case in an appropriate court, such as one in North Carolina, where ACC headquarters were located. But Blumenthal, as Connecticut Attorney General, was incapable of bringing such a suit in a foreign state; he needed a Connecticut forum if he were to remain at the forefront of the case. So rather than allowing the schools to litigate in another state on their own, Blumenthal refiled his case in Connecticut, this time suing the ACC directors and commissioner John Swafford individually. This maneuver was no more successful than the first, and the court once again dismissed the case against those individuals for lack of jurisdiction.

Meanwhile, the legal strategy had backfired. Instead of scaring Miami from leaving the Big East, the litigation angered the Hurricanes, who regarding the lawsuit as a fatal blow to its relationship with the Big East. Miami filed a counterclaim against the University of Connecticut, arguing that Blumenthal's allegations of conspiracies and fraud on the university's behalf were defamatory.

Besides Miami's annoyance and Duke's fright, the Big East schools had nothing to show for their lawsuits. One year into the litigation, no court had even delved into the actual claims made by the attorney general, because he repeatedly brought his cases in the incorrect forum. And in the course of waging this futile war in Connecticut courts, Blumenthal cost the plaintiff schools millions of dollars in legal fees—money that, one might think, would be better spent preparing those schools for the new college football landscape instead of powerlessly inveighing against it.

In the end, the fuss accomplished little. Miami announced on May 31, 2003 that it intended to leave the Big East, and the first, largest domino fell in favor of the ACC. Virginia's threat to withhold support for ACC expansion earned Virginia Tech the second invitation a few weeks later. (Virginia Tech, a plaintiff in Blumenthal's lawsuit, removed itself from the case and the conference simultaneously.)

The litigation's only effect was to delay, briefly, the ACC's manifest destiny towards twelve. The ACC no longer targeted Syracuse; resistance in upstate New York was too staunch for further inquiry. Boston College and its access to Northeastern television markets was the now-obvious 12th choice, but the ACC cooled on the Eagles while Blumenthal's litigation was pending, since it was unclear whether Blumenthal could proceed against Boston College in Connecticut courts.

Determined to change leagues, Boston College secured a declaratory judgment from Massachusetts's highest court clearing the school of any of the wrongdoing alleged by Blumenthal. With that insurance secured, the ACC extended an invitation to Boston College in October—five months after Miami and Virginia Tech, and too late to allow Boston College to leave in time for 2004, but nonetheless getting the ACC its coveted twelfth team.

The dying embers of Blumenthal's litigation smoldered a few more months before extinguishing. The ACC, Miami, and Boston College settled their case with the Big East in 2005 for $5 million— not much more than the combined exit fee would have been anyway—with some of that compensation coming in the form of now-ACC teams playing road games at Big East venues.

***

Despite the blow dealt by the ACC, reports of the Big East's death were premature. The conference was still on the right side of the BCS line, and would remain so for at least a couple years until the conference-strength metrics used to assign automatic qualifying spots were reassessed. In the meantime, the Big East regrouped. Though weakened, there still sat beneath the Big East a ready supply of schools anxious to move to a major conference, even if the Big East was now a bit less major than the others.

Television markets, as always since 1984, were the predominant factor in the Big East's expansion. Louisville, the last team left out of the 1990 round of expansion, was the first team invited to the Big East. The University of Cincinnati gained the Big East access to another mid-sized Midwestern city, while the University of South Florida provided an outlet to the quickly growing Tampa region. Basketball-only members Marquette and DePaul gave the Big East (tenuous) holds in Milwaukee and Chicago, areas traditionally thought of as Big Ten territory. Conference USA, the main victim of the Big East's expansion, claimed that the Northeastern conference was guilty of the same transgressions Robert Blumenthal had claimed against the ACC. This appeal to principle somehow failed to move the Big East.

The new additions left the Big East looking unlike any other major conference. The idea that conferences should be confined to a limited geographic area vanished entirely. Louisville stretched the Big East almost to the banks of the Mississippi River, far away from New England and the Mid-Atlantic. Before the changes, Virginia Tech was the southernmost Big East member; Tampa is 750 miles south of Blacksburg. Big East schools now could be found in twelve states, plus the District of Columbia. If the Big East couldn't woo the most popular teams in one particular region, maybe it could survive by capturing the second or third-most popular teams in several different regions.

***

Down in the ACC, expansion did not have the desired results.

After months of wrangling, the ACC settled upon internal divisions completely untethered from geography. Where the Big 12 had split into North and South Divisions, and the SEC into East and West Divisions, the ACC split into Atlantic and Coastal Divisions (the conference did not explain how a school might be Atlantic without being coastal, or vice versa). In accordance with the wishes of the North Carolina schools, the ACC adopted these divisions for football only.

Shrewdly, it seemed, the ACC split Miami and Florida State into different divisions, but guaranteed one cross-divisional rivalry game per season. Thus, Miami and Florida State would continue their annual rivalry, plus, because they could (and likely would, it was thought) win their divisions, those schools could meet again in the ACC Championship Game. The ACC accordingly scheduled its first five championship games in Florida, preparing for the inevitable Seminoles-Hurricanes matchup.

After seven years, we are still waiting. Neither Florida nor Miami have enjoyed their previous success since the merger. Florida State has played in only two ACC Championship Games, while Miami has played in none. Still worse, because the game was scheduled in Florida in anticipation of that matchup, fans from the teams that actually made the championship game did not attend. The 2008 game in particular, between Boston College and Virginia Tech, drew national derision after fewer than 28,000 fans showed up. Only once, in 2011, have two ACC teams attended BCS bowls, and ACC teams are 1–8 in BCS games since 2004 (the one win came over a Big East team). No ACC team has played in the national championship game since the conference's expansion.

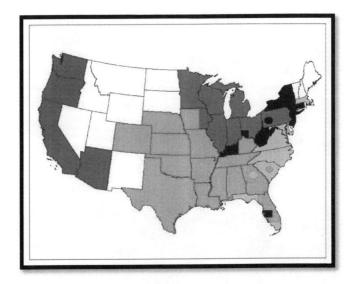

The college football world in 2006. Virginia has returned to being all ACC with the addition of Virginia Tech, but more states than ever—seven—are split between major conferences. For the first time, many schools are geographically isolated within their conferences: Boston College is several states removed from next-closest rival Maryland, while South Florida is hundreds of miles away from Louisville and West Virginia. Non-football conference members and minor conferences are not included on the map.

Epilogue

College football is today undergoing a new revolution, an upheaval broader than that of the early 1990s or 2003. One could write—and no doubt, someday, one will write—a book on the events of the past five years or so. Unfortunately, that story is still being written, and no one can truthfully say that he knows when or how the current revolution will end.

Still, this book would be incomplete without an accounting of what has happened so far, with the added caveat that there is much we do not yet know—about what is to come, and what has already passed.

***

Big Ten commissioner Jim Delany met with ESPN negotiator Mark Shapiro in April 2004. The topics officially under discussion were trifling—Shapiro and Delany were going to chat about ESPN's assignment of broadcasters and scheduling for the upcoming season—but about an hour into the conversation, Delany broached the topic of a contract extension with ESPN. The current television contract was not set to expire until after the 2006 season, but prices for college football games had grown since the Big Ten signed the current deal. Delany hoped that he could offer his conference to ESPN long-term in return for a better deal now.

Shapiro, a notoriously ruthless negotiator, would have none of it. The Big Ten had three years left on its current deal, and his network was unwilling to bind itself to an expensive, lengthy contract with a partner disposed to renegotiation should the terms no longer suit them. If the Big Ten wanted an extension, it could have one for the current contract terms. After a few minutes of back and forth, Shapiro curtly cautioned Delany, "take it or leave it. If you don't take our offer you are rolling the dice."

"Consider them rolled."

Two years later, the Big Ten—in conjunction with Fox Television—announced a new project: the Big Ten Network ("BTN"). For the first time in college football history, a conference would control its own television network, cutting out the traditional middleman. Before, conferences negotiated with television networks, which in turn negotiated with advertisers and (in ESPN's case) cable carriers. Now, the Big Ten would be responsible for finding its own advertisers and negotiating its own carriage rates with cable providers.

The project was fraught with potential pratfalls. No conference had ever before negotiated directly with cable carriers or advertisers. Fox Entertainment Group held a 49 percent share in BTN, so at least a substantial partner in the project would have some expertise in those areas, but the contract price collapse following *NCAA v. University of Oklahoma* was a warning against conferences stepping too far outside of their institutional know-how. Television networks, without question, had outmaneuvered the conferences in the first few rounds of negotiation following the Supreme Court decision. Now, the Big Ten hoped they would succeed in their very first battle with cable companies, despite the negative precedent.

This proved doubtful at first. The Big Ten demanded placement on the cable carriers' basic subscription package, and not relegation to the "premium" tiers to which so few cable consumers subscribe. Further, the Big Ten wanted $1.10 per cable subscriber, more than any non-sports channel carried by any cable company within the with which they were negotiating.

ESPN can demand such high carriage fees for itself—much higher carriage fees, actually—because ESPN broadcasts major events year-round in all the major sports. BTN wasn't even going to show all of the Big Ten's football and basketball games; indeed, the most valuable, highest profile games would still be sold to national networks or ESPN. Rather, BTN would show a few dozen of the conference's less important football games, all of which were broadcast entirely during fifteen or so Saturdays during the fall. Men's basketball was another valuable asset for BTN, and basketball covered more dates and times than football, but the network would still be left with thousands upon thousands of hours to fill. How many cable subscribers would be interested in paying $1.10 a month for Northwestern volleyball and Purdue swimming?

BTN debuted one day before the start of the 2007 college football season, but few viewers were able to watch. The conference reached an agreement with satellite provider DirecTV before the games kicked off, but every major cable carrier in the Midwest declined to pick up BTN. Throughout the academic year, cable companies and the Big Ten played chicken, each thinking that frustrated fans who missed Division I-AA Appalachian State defeat #5 Michigan (for just one example) would turn against the other side first. With few viewers came even fewer advertisers, and what few fans could watch BTN were treated to a seemingly endless stream of commercials for shaving cream, canned tomatoes, and agricultural products.

The 2007–08 academic year passed with neither the Big Ten nor the cable carriers backing down. But in June 2008, the first and largest carrier cracked. Comcast, which did business in seven of the eight Big Ten states and controlled roughly 60 percent of the cable market within the conference's geographic footprint, agreed to pay $.70 per subscriber for BTN—less than the $1.10 the Big Ten had sought, but far more than Comcast paid to almost every other network it carried. Once Comcast fell, the other cable networks quickly scrambled behind; none could risk losing subscribers to the market leader because of stubbornness over BTN.

With cable networks now finally on board, BTN gained momentum. The network turned a profit during its second year in existence. By the 2009–10 academic year, the network returned $7 million to each of its eleven schools, a figure that accounted for one-third of Big Ten athletic departments' total revenue. The Big Ten's separation from television networks was not complete — a television network owned 49 percent of BTN, after all, and the conference still sold games to ESPN — but the conference had shown that preexisting television networks were not the essential component once assumed, reaping a multi-million dollar reward in so showing.

Commissioner Delany responded to the success of BTN in two ways. First he sent a bottle of champagne to Mark Shapiro, who dumped the sparkling wine down the drain. Second, in December 2009, Delany announced that the Big Ten was once again exploring expansion. Twenty years after adopting Penn State, it was time to close the Notre Dame-sized hole in the eleven team conference's membership.

***

The Big Ten won just a single national championship between 2000 and 2010 (Ohio State in 2002). The Big 12 won two national championships in that decade (Oklahoma in 2000, Texas in 2005), more than any conference except the SEC. Yet while the SEC and Big Ten raked in massive television contracts, the Big 12 languished. Despite respectable accomplishments on the field, the conference was only marginally successful economically.

Financial success in the SEC and Big Ten came differently. The Big Ten, the nation's oldest athletic conference, was situated over fertile television territory. After the addition of Penn State in 1990, Philadelphia, Pittsburgh, Cleveland, Cincinnati, Detroit, Indianapolis, Chicago, and Milwaukee all fell within Big Ten states, not to mention the often respectably sized cities in which the schools actually sat (Columbus, Minneapolis, and Madison, for example). The Big Ten may have struggled on the field compared to the SEC or Big 12, but its population provided an advantage each time a television contract came up for renegotiation.

The SEC, located in the more sparsely populated Deep South, contained fewer large television markets, but what the South lacked in numbers it made up in enthusiasm. Professional football was slow in coming to the former Confederacy, and when the NFL did arrive, it came in the form of the usually futile New Orleans Saints and Atlanta Falcons. Although professional football eclipsed the college game everywhere elsewhere, Southerners remained attached to their sport (the six national championships between 2000 and 2010 couldn't have hurt, either).

Meanwhile, the Big 12's fans lacked both the numbers and the enthusiasm of their rival conferences. The problems that plagued the SWC in its last days, and thus led to the creation of the Big 12, never really disappeared. Adding the states of Oklahoma, Kansas, Nebraska, Iowa, and Colorado did not add many major television markets besides Denver. Nor are the states of Kansas and Colorado famous for being crazy about college football.

Texas *is* crazy about college football, of course, but that presented its own problems. Rather than an even distribution of interest across the conference, the Big 12 was dominated by a few major schools, with the remainder struggling to fill their stadiums to half-capacity. While Kansas and Iowa State meandered through irrelevancy, Texas football earned more revenue than any team in college sports.

The Big 12 coped with this inequality by enshrining it. Most major conferences provided for an equal distribution of television revenue. If the Big Ten Network made $100 million, the eleven teams of the conference earned a little over $9 million apiece. Conversely, the Big 12 handled contract matters much as the NCAA and CFA had before: more valuable teams were entitled to a greater share of the pie, which further divided the upper from the lower class.

Unequal television revenue almost killed the NCAA, and it did kill the CFA. Now, inequality threatened the Big 12. The lower class of the Big 12 disliked the disparity, but could not do much about it; no other conferences were clamoring for Baylor or Iowa State football. Like SMU or Rice during the SMU's final gasps, those schools' best chance to survive was sticking with the Big 12, whether the revenue agreement was "fair" or not. The conference's upper-middle class, on the other hand, had options. Those teams despised the growing Texas hegemony over the conference, fearing that the Longhorns' burgeoning finances would turn the conference into the Big One and Little Eleven.

Especially upset was Nebraska, whose disagreements with Texas extended back to the founding of the Big 12. Unlike the other conference expansions of the time, the Big 12 was supposed to be a merger of two now-defunct conferences, but Nebraska officials viewed this as mere face-saving on behalf of its new Lone Star brethren. The SWC, not the Big Eight, was being torn apart by rivals. The SWC, not the Big Eight, had been forced to jettison unproductive programs. The SWC, not the Big Eight, was competitively irrelevant before the 1996 merger; Nebraska had just won the national championship in 1994 and 1995, would win another in 1997, and fellow former Big Eight member Oklahoma claimed the crown in 2000. By the turn of the century, the SWC national championship drought stood at thirty years and counting. Yet from the beginning, Nebraska felt its grasp over the new conference slipping. When the Big 12 divided into North and South Divisions, Nebraska was separated from decades-long rival Oklahoma. Texas would get to continue its Rid River Rivalry with the Sooners just as it had in the past, while Nebraska would have to be content playing Oklahoma every other year.

Another point of contention was the location of the Big 12 Championship Game. From the conference's creation in 1996 until 2008, the game oscillated between north and south each season: in

Texas one year, then Kansas City or St. Louis the next. Following the 2009 construction of the new Cowboys Stadium in Arlington, however, the Big 12 semi-permanently moved the championship game to Texas. Cowboys Stadium would host, at minimum, the next five conference championships, and there was nothing to stop stadium owner Jerry Jones from bidding for the event once again when the contract was through.

Finally, as always, there was money. Nebraska does not contain any large television markets, but it does boast a large and dedicated fan base, much like the SEC (Nebraska has sold out every home game since 1962). But even with those advantages, Nebraska could never hope to keep up with the Texas football revenue machine, and the unequal Big 12 revenue distribution threatened to make that divide permanent. The merger had turned into a noose.

***

Out on the West Coast, new Pac-10 commissioner Larry Scott sensed an opportunity. His conference had mostly sat out the revolution of the early 1990s, neither threatening nor threatened during that period. The Rocky Mountains that insulated the Pac-10 were a blessing and a curse. Any conference looking to poach a Pac-10 team would commit itself to repeatedly crossing the continental divide through the course of the year, a costly enterprise when one takes into account the many non-revenue teams that would be forced to make the trip out west. And even if a thieving conference could overcome the geographic divide, the rivalries and shared history of the Pac-10 made that conference unlikely to be fissured.

On the other hand, the Rockies had also made expansion difficult *for* the Pac-10. The states immediately adjacent to the Pac-10—Idaho, Nevada, and New Mexico—were sparsely populated and contained no major football programs. Apart from the smooching corners of Arizona and Colorado, no Pac-10 state bordered another state that held a team from a major conference.

Historically, the only program of any significance between the West Coast and the Great Plains was BYU, the 1984 national champion and spiritual home to American Mormons. With its national following, inviting BYU made economic sense, and poaching the MWC would be easier than stealing a team away from a BCS conference. But BYU presented its own difficulties. Like the Big Ten with Notre Dame, Pac-10 leaders doubted whether BYU was a comfortable fit with the conference's mostly public, entirely secular members. BYU athletes do not play sports on Sunday, which is not much of an issue for the football program but causes headaches for all the other teams. And academic leaders doubted that BYU's graduate programs were sufficient to support Pac-10 membership. BYU was thus a nonstarter.

For decades, however, the Mormon university had been losing its iron grip on the Beehive State, relinquishing popularity to rival Utah. Unlike BYU, the University of Utah was secular and focused on graduate-level education. Utah also was located in Salt Lake City, one of the few major television markets in the region.

Plus, Utah was *good*. After decades of languishing behind their Holy War rivals BYU, Utah established itself as perhaps the premier minor-conference team of the 2000s. The 2004 Utah squad is one of only two minor-conference teams ever to be favored over a major-conference team in a BCS bowl game, obliterating Pittsburgh in the Fiesta Bowl 35–7. A few years later, Utah would return to the BCS, this time defeating Alabama in the Sugar Bowl and finishing the 2008 season undefeated.

Convincing Utah to abandon the MWC would be easy, but twelve was the magic number for expansion, since NCAA bylaws require twelve teams in a conference to hold a conference championship game. Just that single additional game meant millions of dollars in extra revenue for the conference. If a logical dance partner could be found, the Pac-10 would not stop with

Utah at eleven teams as the Big Ten had done with Penn State in 1990.

***

The surest test of a conference's strength is the response of its membership to expansion rumors. When the Big Ten announced that it was considering adding a twelfth team, the SEC and Pac-10 did not bat an eye. Conversely, the ACC, Big East, and Big 12 each worried that it might become victims of the Big Ten. Those fears set off a vicious cycle. No team wanted to be the last wedded to a doomed arrangement, and failure to jump at an opportunity could leave marginal BCS conference teams in the same position Houston, Rice, SMU, and TCU had found themselves when the SWC disbanded. Once fellow conference mates were caught with wandering eyes, fellow members began seeking affairs of their own.

Early in the process, the presumed soon-to-be victim of the Big Ten was the Big East. Although the weakest of the major conferences after the ACC's 2003 raid, the Big East still had a few assets worth taking; Syracuse, for example, had been a prime target of the ACC before being cajoled by Virginia into accepting Virginia Tech instead of the Orange. With only eight football-playing schools, losing even a single program could kill the Big East. But when the Big Ten studied its options, each of the Big East targets had flaws. Pittsburgh was already within territory covered by the Big Ten Network, so adding the nearby school would do little to improve the conference's economic situation. Syracuse was rather far away, and its football program was not particularly popular even inside New York. Rutgers was further away still, and while adding Rutgers might get BTN added by New York City cable carriers, it might not; if the Big Ten expanded to New Jersey and could not establish a cable presence, the conference would have just voluntarily given away one-twelfth of its revenue in return for a program that hadn't been relevant since beating Princeton in 1869.

More valuable prizes lied west of the Mississippi River. Missouri, one of the many teams disappointed with the Big 12's financial arrangement, all but publicly lobbied for an invitation from the Big Ten, though as with Pittsburgh, BTN had already infiltrated Missouri's television markets. Even Texas—the impetus for Big 12 destabilization—was rumored to be participating in talks with the Big Ten, though it is unclear how the two sides could ever have reached an agreement given how firmly the concept of equal revenue sharing was enmeshed in Big Ten culture.

While the college football world waited for the Big Ten to choose its next partner, the Pac-10 struck first. Colorado, like the rest of the Big 12, had been frightened by the instability of the conference. Missouri was looking to exit; Texas A&M would leave if they could find a partner; Texas was exploring its options. Rather than later reacting to the departure of one of those schools—when safe departure might be too late—Colorado secured a stable home for itself first.

Utah's previous defection to the Pac-10 was, in the grand scheme of things, not that big of a deal—major conferences had stolen teams from minor conferences since time immemorial. But Colorado's departure to the Pac-10 (now dubbed the Pac-12) was zero-sum: one major conference's gain was another's loss. The Pac-12 had strengthened itself at the expense of the Big 12, which, now weakened, would struggle to defend itself against the predators tearing it apart.

Missouri desperately sought admission to the Big Ten, but that conference was hunting larger game: Nebraska. Colorado's departure made the Big 12 that much more unbearably Texas-centric. One of Nebraska's few remaining rivalries from the Big Eight was now broken. The last such rivalry might end at any time with Missouri's exit. The financial disparities driving these rivals into the arms of other conferences hurt Nebraska as much as any Big 12 program.

Nebraska was not yet on the Big Ten's radar, however. When the Big Ten commissioned a report examining which potential invitees made the most economic sense, Nebraska had not even been among the teams studied. The Cornhuskers were a longshot to leave the Big 12, it was thought, and time spent chasing Nebraska could be better used pursuing partners that were more realistic.

All that changed with the impending departure of Colorado. Nebraska understood—and the Big Ten knew that Nebraska understood—that the Big 12 might not remain a stable home for long. Within two weeks following Colorado's withdrawal from the Big 12, the Big Ten and Nebraska jointly announced that the conference had offered, and the school had accepted, an invitation to join. In less than a month, the Big 12 had lost its two most valuable northern programs.

***

The remaining Big 12 members split into two groups. First, there were the programs which were likely safe regardless of what happened to the conference—Texas, Texas A&M, Oklahoma, and probably Oklahoma State. These programs were valuable enough that they could find homes elsewhere should the Big 12 disintegrate. In the other group were programs like Iowa State, Kansas, and Kansas State, which might not have a seat when the music stopped. The groups were clear at the extremes but blurry at the margins; Missouri, for example—so recently rebuffed by the Big Ten—could not be entirely sure whether it would be saved, but Mizzou was not in as dire straits as, say, Iowa State.

Though the first group was ultimately safe, regardless of what might happen during realignment, it was these teams most desperately looking to leave. Iowa State and the other Big 12 also-rans *needed* the conference to hold together, and were willing to agree to whatever conditions were necessary to remain sitting at the adults' table. But just as Nebraska had left the Big 12 frustrated by its declining share of the revenue split, the remaining upper-middle class of the conference was most frustrated by Texas's hegemony. Texas A&M quite openly courted the SEC as a suitor, while Missouri's willingness to leave the conference had been clear for months.

Finally, Scott and the Pac-12 looked to put the Big 12 out of its misery. The Pac-12 entered negotiations with Texas, Oklahoma, Oklahoma State, and Texas Tech, hoping to fashion a "superconference" from the juiciest entrails of the Big 12. Sixteen-team superconferences had been a popular media subject since the 1990s realignment, but never before had a conference actually taken steps towards making one a reality. By September 2011, media reports indicated that the deal was all but completed.

But the agreement was never as close as was reported. The unbreakable snag, once again, was Texas. Since the departure of Nebraska, Texas had announced the creation of the Longhorn Network ("LHN"), a television network much like the BTN but focused entirely on Texas athletics. The Big 12 revenue agreement allowed Texas to pursue this project, and also allowed Texas to fully retain whatever benefits resulted from LHN. Wedded to its hegemony over the Big 12, Texas could never agree to a conference arrangement that did not permit the Longhorns to pursue projects such as LHN or maintain its economic superiority. The Pac-12, for its part, was far too attached to its equal distribution of revenue to allow exceptions for new members. Without Texas's participation, the Pac-12 was uninterested in bringing on so many mouths to feed at once, and by October, the deal was officially dead. If superconferences were inevitable, they would have to wait a while longer.

***

Maybe not much longer, though. With the Pac-12's proposal and (in September 2011) seemingly successful move to the superconference model, other conferences began feeling as though they had been caught flat-footed. If superconferences were coming—and breathless media reports assured everyone that they were—then administrators had to act quick, lest they be left with little from which to choose.

The SEC's next move was rather obvious. Initially, SEC leaders had been only lukewarm towards Texas A&M's overtures, but with the Pac-12's maneuvering, A&M was an obvious first addition in the push towards sixteen. There was no question Texas A&M wanted out of the Big 12, so the SEC did not fear being publicly rebuffed by the Aggies. Furthermore, Texas A&M would give the SEC inroads into the massive Dallas and Houston television markets. While the Pac-12/Big 12 saga was still unfolding, the SEC took the plunge, extending an offer to Texas A&M to become the thirteenth member of the conference.

Fearing for the safety of its own members now that the SEC was expanding, the nearby ACC looked to solidify its own position. Having raided the Big East once already in 2003, poaching Northeastern teams was becoming routine for the conference, and the ACC returned to that well once again. Without public prelude or fanfare, the ACC announced in late-September 2011 that Syracuse and Pittsburgh had accepted offers to join the conference. That Pittsburgh was willing to jump to the ACC was unsurprising. But Syracuse had resisted the ACC's siren song less than a decade before, and Jim Boeheim was no less powerful in the Syracuse athletic department than he had been in 2003. But he was also aging, and like Penn State with Joe Paterno in 1989, Syracuse had begun planning for a future without its leader. However much affection the school might towards the Big

East, the ACC had something more important than affection—money.

These maneuvers filtered down through the lower conferences, each domino toppling another. The Big East, now with only six football programs, was desperate to restock its ranks. In time, it would extend offers to teams wherever it could find them—Houston, University of Central Florida, San Diego State, Boise State, Temple, SMU, TCU, and Memphis. Few of these programs were well established or even very popular in their regions, but the Big East, with its survival at stake, could not afford to be choosy.

This nationwide approach to conference building was bold—the Big East now stretched from Connecticut to Florida and from New Jersey to San Diego—but it was not enough to calm the nerves of its remaining stalwart members. UConn openly campaigned for, and was openly rejected by, the ACC, which still resented Richard Blumenthal's lawsuits almost a decade later. The Big 12, scrambling after the loss of Texas A&M, grabbed West Virginia. It also stole TCU before the Horned Frogs had played a single game in the Big East. Not only were marriages dissolving, but engagements were breaking before relationships could be consummated.

As the Big 12 stole from the Big East, the SEC stole from the Big 12. Looking to avoid an awkward thirteen-team setup, the SEC offered Missouri the safety raft the Tigers had sought for so long. With Missouri's defection, the Big 12 had lost one-third of its 2009 membership within two years. But the Big 12 had at least dodged the bullet aimed for its heart fired by the Pac-12 and remained reasonably competitive at ten teams.

By the time all had settled, four of the other five conferences had grown—the Pac-12 and Big Ten to twelve teams, the ACC and SEC to fourteen—while the fifth, the Big East, masked its infirmity with geographic scope.

As bad as things look for the Big East, no conference fared worse than the WAC. When the Pac-10 grabbed Utah from the Mountain West Conference, it looked as though the MWC might be the minor conference to suffer most from realignment. And, for a fleeting moment in August 2010, the WAC looked as though it had sprung a coup, stealing BYU from the MWC. But that victory was short-lived. The MWC, in turn, stole Boise State, Fresno State, Hawaii, and Nevada—four of the nine WAC members—a few days later. BYU, now walking into a party everyone else was leaving, also abandoned the WAC, declaring independence rather than sheepishly returning to the MWC. Like rats on a sinking ship, the remaining WAC members looked for homes wherever it could find them—Conference USA, even the lowly Sun Belt Conference—while the WAC resorted to offering invitations to football programs that had launched only within the last decade. This frantic maneuvering to remain part of Division I-A seems unlikely to be successful, and the WAC—once strong enough to belong to the CFA, once home to national champion BYU— currently appears to be on its final breaths.

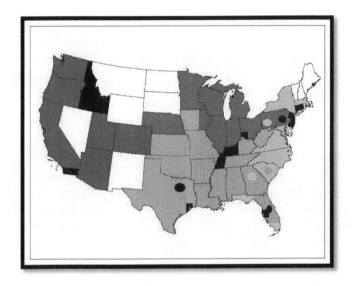

The college football world in 2014, if all schools and conferences follow through on their current (September 2012) contract obligations. The Big East stretches from Connecticut to Florida to Idaho to California, while the Big 12 skips over multiple states to West Virginia. In 1980, one state had teams from more than one major conference. By 1996, that number had grown to six, and by 2006 than number was seven. In 2014, ten states have teams from multiple conferences, with Florida, Texas, and Pennsylvania split three ways. Three of the six conferences are no longer located in contiguous states. As before, this map does not take non-football conference members or minor conferences into account.

***

The BCS was structured around the concept of six coequal conferences. That idea was already flimsy by 2003, by which time many of the Big East's strongest football programs had defected to the ACC. By 2011, with the Big East left in tatters and scrambling across the country to convince whatever football program it could to join, the concept of coequality was dead.

Popular dissatisfaction with the BCS was also growing. Each season seemed to present a new challenge for the two-team playoff concept. In 2008, Utah finished without a loss and defeated Alabama in the Sugar Bowl, and yet never had a chance to play for the national championship. Ditto TCU in 2010, which defeated Wisconsin in the Rose Bowl after finishing the year without a loss. Finally, in 2011, the national championship game featured — for the first time in BCS history — a game between two teams from the same conference: LSU and Alabama. In fact, those two teams came from the same division in the SEC, and the two had played earlier in the season, with LSU defeating Alabama in Tuscaloosa. Despite Alabama not winning its division or making the SEC championship game, the Crimson Tide was given the invite to the BCS championship game over similar one-loss teams such as Oklahoma State and Stanford. Having been provided that opportunity, Alabama defeated LSU in New Orleans, becoming the first program in modern college football history to win the national championship without winning its conference.

With changes needed to the BCS in any event because of the hobbling of the Big East, and with the public clamoring for a playoff of some sort, the conferences finally inched towards a postseason tournament. Previously, the conferences had been unwilling to dilute the value of their primary product, the regular season. But skyrocketing television contracts and renewed cries for a playoff meant that adding a few additional games to the postseason would potentially result in hundreds of millions in extra revenue each season.

The trick, as before, was ensuring that only the "right" schools—that is, schools from major conferences—would be entitled to a share of the money. Starting in 2014—the year after the ongoing BCS television contract expires—the major conferences will implement a four-team playoff. Teams will be chosen by a selection committee, rather than pollsters or computer programs. Most years, four teams is too few for any programs from minor conferences to sneak through, especially since the best of those programs have been swiped by the major conferences in recent years. Still, the door is technically open to those teams, thus leaving the playoff proposal immune from antitrust challenges.

***

Where is college football headed? Given the immense changes the sport has undergone the past few years, any predictions must be hazarded cautiously, if at all. Rather than offer anything as foolish as firm conclusions, I offer eight questions, the answers to which I believe will determine the direction college football will travel over the coming decades.

1. Is there a sports bubble?

Every American sports league has been blessed by a booming market for sports on television since the turn of the century. Advertisers love that sporting-event viewers are unlikely to record games, which means that sports fans do not fast-forward through commercials. Networks love what advertisers love. The main sports demographic—middle-aged men—is also the key advertising demographic, since in many households, it is middle-aged men who make major spending decisions.

Traditional television network contracts locked leagues (and in college sports, conferences) into a set payout: X dollars over Y number of years. If the network sold extra advertising and made more money than originally expected, that meant more profit for the *network*, not the leagues. On the other hand, if ad sales were worse than expected, the network would eat the loss. During the life of the contract, the networks, not the conferences, bore the risk.

Many professional leagues, including the NFL and NBA, have moved programming away from traditional television networks onto networks owned either partly or entirely by the league. The Big Ten pioneered this process in college sports, launching the Big Ten Network in 2007, and the Pac-12 has recently followed that trend. With the major conferences moving towards ownership models, more of the risk will be borne by the conferences themselves. In a rising market, this means greater profits, since the extra revenue is returned to league coffers.

Can the market rise forever, though? It sure seems like it today, but it wasn't many years ago that the housing market was believed to be impervious to setbacks as well. Athletic programs will begin planning renovations, paying coaches, and taking on debt based on the revenue projections from their television networks. If the markets turn and advertising during sporting events is no longer as valuable, many schools across the country will face significant financial shortfalls. Network ownership alone is not a secret method for minting money, though it has often felt that way and may continue to feel that way for years to come.

Most of the conferences' television revenue still comes from independent cable networks, such as ESPN. But even that source of revenue may not be safe forever. Sports networks can charge a premium to cable carriers because so much of the cable subscriber base turns to cable specifically *because* of the live sports coverage viewers cannot get anywhere else. Still, those sports networks are subsidized by the millions of cable subscribers who have no interest in athletics, yet still silently pay several dollars a month for ESPN as part of their cable bill. If those subscribers abandon cable for on-demand video options, such as Hulu and Netflix, sports networks may be unable to continue paying the massive contracts to which conferences have now become accustomed. A reverse in revenue will require painful readjustments by all sports leagues, not just college football.

2. Does Division I-A still make sense?

In 1988, 105 teams played at the highest level of college football. In 2012, 124 teams played in Division I-A (now officially known as the Football Bowl Subdivision, or FBS). Program inflation does not matter as much as it did back in the day of joint NCAA television contracts, since teams and conferences are left to fend for themselves on the open television market. Small schools might move up to Division I-A, but they are still playing in the small ponds of their minor contracts, still not earning much money, and still not taking major bowl money away from major teams.

On the other hand, the addition of every new team to Division I-A dilutes the value of college football a bit more. The major conferences schedule eight or nine conference games, and because conferences aim for competitive balance, there is a reasonable assurance that much of the schedule will be interesting. But schools are left on their own when it comes to non-conference scheduling. Many teams eschew competitive games for low-level patsies. As much as a third of a team's schedule can be made up of these weak teams—or, to put it another way—as much as a third of the potential value of college football is lost each season to weak scheduling and matchups practically no one wants to see.

Meanwhile, those teams making up the bottom level of Division I-A struggle to stay afloat. Most could not break even without significant financial support from their school, usually in the form of a fee added to the tuition bill of every student at the university. These teams also depend on payments from larger schools; in return, the weaker schools rent themselves out for road game beatings. Come postseason, smaller schools pay hundreds of thousands of dollars in transportation fees to play in bowl games attended by fewer than 10,000 fans.

Even with college football flush with cash unlike ever before, the survival of these teams is in danger. Furthermore, it is unclear why these teams *should* survive if they are unable to support themselves and are dependent upon school or government subsidies, apart from as a way of boosting the pride of a handful of alumni. If the bottom half of Division I-A disappeared tomorrow, or was relegated to a lower division, the remaining matchups would be better and fans would be treated to several dozen better quality matchups each year. But can major programs wean themselves off unbalanced home-away schedules and easy victories?

3. Are the Northwesterns and Vanderbilts of the world safe?

Four major conference teams—Houston, Rice, TCU, and SMU—were relegated into mid-major purgatory when the SWC exploded in the mid-1990s. Baylor just barely survived the axe. More recently, Kansas, Kansas State, and Iowa State were threatened with irrelevancy when the Big 12 nearly split apart. Membership in major conferences is not eternal, and conferences are still economic arrangements above all else.

A few teams, however, have been shielded from this economic reality. As the most stable and financially successful conferences, the Big Ten and SEC have never had to reevaluate their membership rolls. But in a more cutthroat competitive environment, perpetually unsuccessful schools with small fan bases may no longer be welcome. At a minimum, more powerful and successful schools within those conferences may reevaluate whether their conferences should remain a collection of equals, with all television revenue being split evenly, or whether conference members should become something more like Animal Farm equals—that is, some teams a little more equal than others.

Now, schools such as Northwestern and Vanderbilt do provide plenty to their conferences. Both schools are academic stalwarts. Both schools are founding members of their conference. Then again, Rice was a founding member of the SWC, and is a pretty darn good academic school to boot, but that did not save them when difficult membership decisions needed to be made.

Someone will always be on the bottom of the totem pole. Moreover, competitive balance is not stationary. The University of Chicago was once a major football power. Oregon was quite recently a very marginal program. A few "major" teams remain in place today mostly on the strength of accomplishments earned before most of their fans had been born. Economic chaos threatens those schools, whose merits will be reevaluated out of necessity by their competitive betters should their own safety be threatened.

4. Is the next move further expansion, or independence?

A world with fewer and larger conferences has been the presumed future of college football for well over two decades. John Mackovic, head coach of Illinois in 1990 and later head coach of Texas and Arizona, offered what was then the conventional wisdom: "It wouldn't surprise me by the year 2000 if we have only three or four major conferences with a realignment of schools and divisions. The conferences will be larger. You might have twenty-team leagues." Why was expansion inevitable? "We've already begun to look at the future of TV in college athletics. It is generating a lot of income for colleges. It might be easier to establish TV coverage in one large conference than in putting together two or three smaller conferences."

The year 2000 came and went without superconferences (except for the quickly aborted sixteen-team WAC). But we have moved closer to the supposed endgame. The Big Ten expanded from eleven to twelve teams with the addition of Nebraska. The Pac-10 has become the Pac-12. The SEC expanded from ten (at the time of Mackovic's comment), to twelve with the addition of Arkansas and South Carolina, to fourteen today. The ACC has gone from nine to fourteen teams in less than a decade. Perhaps the process has taken longer than originally anticipated, but if you follow the trend out only a bit further, the world of the superconference will have arrived.

At some point, though, expansion stops making sense. Every team added to a conference is another mouth to feed. Most of the major conferences share television revenue evenly. Adding four teams to a twelve-team conference is a losing proposition if one-sixteenth of the new television contract is not worth more than one-twelfth of the old contract. The move that almost every major conference has made from ten to twelve teams added a discrete event—a conference championship game—that could not otherwise exist. There is no similar boost in revenue for expanding from twelve to sixteen; the gains must come from added interest in the league.

Meanwhile, the teams at the very top of the pyramid—Texas, Michigan, Alabama, and so on—create a disproportionate share of the television revenue within their conference. Their games appear on television more often and have higher ratings than Baylor, Indiana, and Kentucky games. Longstanding cultural bonds keep teams like Michigan and Ohio State safely within the Big Ten. The same can be said for Alabama, Florida, and the like in the SEC.

That may not be true everywhere. The Big Ten has been around since the 19th century, and the SEC since the 1930s, but the Big 12 was a creature of the mid-1990s. Only three of the SWC schools that merged with the Big Eight to create the Big 12 remain in the conference today. And Texas, one of those schools, does not have strong cultural ties to the other two remaining schools, Texas Tech and Baylor. A fourth SWC team, TCU, joined the Big 12 in 2012, but TCU's ties with Texas were not even strong enough to save the Horned Frogs from relegation when the SWC disintegrated.

Given Texas's lack of history with the schools in its conference, little is holding the Longhorns in the Big 12 other than economic self-interest. Whereas Kansas and Iowa State need Texas and the Big 12, lest they be cast off without a safety net, Texas only stays within the Big 12 only because the math currently works for them. And the math only works for the Longhorns because the Big 12, unlike the SEC or Big Ten, does not split television revenue evenly. Instead, like the CFA television contracts or the central NCAA television contracts, the Big 12 attempts to distribute television money roughly in proportion with how teams "deserve" that money. If the lesser members of the conference attempted to force a more even distribution, Texas might depart to a conference that allowed the Longhorns to continue earning a larger share of television revenue.

Or, Texas might simply abandon the conference project entirely. Notre Dame has shown that long-term independence is still a realistic strategy. When Notre Dame receives a paycheck from NBC for its television games, the school need not split that money with anyone. Eyeing that arrangement, and buoyed by the success of the Big Ten Network, Texas announced the creation of the Longhorn Network in 2011. With LHN, the University of Texas has a vehicle that circumvents traditional conference contracts for broadcasting games and secondary programming, allowing Texas to avoid sharing any of the money earned on the network with anyone else.

Unfortunately for Texas (and perhaps fortunately for everyone else in the Big 12), LHN has been a bit of a disaster since its inception. Most cable carriers have refused to broadcast the network, citing the lack of programming and the high carrier fees that Texas is requesting. Texas's partnership with ESPN in creating LHN has drawn criticism from sports fans and media critics, who charge that the station is unduly interfering with the structure of college sports. And many athletic departments— inside and outside the Big 12—resent what they perceive as Texas's unwillingness to play nice for the greater good.

Even if LHN fails, however, the underlying economic realities that led to LHN's launch will not change. There will always be a few elite athletic programs at the pinnacle of the sport, and those programs will seek to earn revenue in line with their importance. These dynamics nearly led the CFA to secede from the NCAA, and did lead the CFA to bring federal antitrust claims all the way to the Supreme Court. Later, that interplay between the top schools in the CFA and the remaining organization caused the CFA's disintegration. That process may soon play out within athletic conferences as well.

Further, although the LHN may be a failure up to this point, there is no reason to think schools cannot discover how to make an independent television station work in the future. BYUtv, the home network of Brigham Young University, is available to over sixty-million cable subscribers throughout the United States, though in most places a special additional subscription is needed to access BYUtv. Brigham Young has some advantages over many independent or potentially independent schools; like Notre Dame, BYU has millions of co-religionists to call upon across the country, and thus interest in BYU is not necessarily limited to alumni and those in the immediate geographic area. Much of the programming on BYUtv is not oriented around sports or the school, but religious programming promoted by the Church of Jesus Christ of Latter-day Saints. This is an advantage only a very small number of schools could hope to leverage.

But even taking account the peculiarities of its situation, BYU has shown that an independent television network need not be a disaster, and it may only be a matter of time before some other Texas-like institution decides to try the project. If that school is successful, superconferences may go extinct before they are ever born.

5. Is the bowl postseason model endangered?

College football's postseason is unique. Instead of a playoff run by a central organization, successful teams attend bowl games arranged by private groups. Some of those bowls, such as the Rose Bowl, offer significant payouts to competing teams, and attendance at those games is considered a major accomplishment. Others, such as the Beef O'Brady's Bowl or the Kraft Fight Hunger Bowl, not so much. All these games, however, high and low, are cut from the same economic cloth, and the peculiar bowl system has survived for over a century.

This may soon be changing. Many fans have complained that there are simply too many games rewarding too many teams. Making a bowl game is no longer the accomplishment it once was. In 2011, 70 out of 120 teams attended bowl games, including one team with a losing record during the regular season. Six victories are needed to make a bowl game, and one of those victories may come over a Division I-AA squad, so teams need only go 5–6 against Division I-A competition to make the postseason.

This bowl inflation would be relatively harmless if not for the immense cost to the schools attending the lowest bowls. Attendance at the aforementioned Beef O'Brady's Bowl was reported at just a hair over 20,000 in 2011, and those who watched or attended the game may be forgiven for believing that number to be inflated. Bowl promoters require competing teams to guarantee ticket sales; Florida International and Marshall, the 2011 Beef O'Brady's Bowl competitors, were required to buy five-thousand tickets apiece. Low-level schools rarely come close to selling their allotment. When Nevada made the Hawai'i Bowl in 2011, it sold ten tickets from its allotment. The Nevada athletic department ate the cost of the remainder of the tickets, donating the vast majority to charities. Between these ticket guarantees and the cost of travel, many low-level teams lose hundreds of thousands of dollars during postseason play. And yet the schools still attend, because turning down a bowl invitation is tantamount to announcing that if you attend Western State U, you will never play in the postseason.

(Much has been made of high-level teams "breaking even" on prestigious bowl trips, but this is an unfair criticism. First, many of these teams split bowl revenue with their conference, so although they only earn one-tenth or one-twelfth of their own bowl payout, they also earn that same fraction of the revenue from every other game, and these figures are often not factored back by muckraking journalists into the cost-benefit analysis. Second, and more importantly, top schools don't treat major bowls as a revenue opportunity, but instead as a reward for all those associated with the team. Players, cheerleaders, band members, athletic department representatives, and many others spend several days in beautiful hotels, all on the school's dime. Teams are provided ample sight-seeing opportunities, again paid for by the school. If these programs wanted to cut the fat from their budget, they could easily do so. These schools lose money in the same way you lose money every time you go on vacation. Profit maximization isn't the point of vacations, and major athletic departments reasonably have decided it is not the point of bowl games, either.)

The tradition of private management of the college football postseason is changing in two ways. First, the introduction of a four-team postseason, beginning in 2014, threatens to render the bowl games—even the games near the top of the food chain— comparatively meaningless. The Rose Bowl has always been an inherent reward for Big Ten and Pac-8/10/12 teams, but will it remain so in years where the champions of those leagues cannot make the playoff? Each expansion of the playoff absorbs further interest from the remaining bowls. If a four-team playoff does not kill the bowls, an eight-team or sixteen-team playoff might succeed.

Second, conferences are wrestling ownership of bowls away from private entities. The college football postseason tournament will take place within the preexisting bowl structure, but conferences are dictating to the bowls which teams will be chosen for those games. Even further down the chain, conferences are avoiding the private groups entirely where they can. The SEC and Big 12 conferences, for example, announced in 2012 a "Champions Bowl" that will be managed entirely by those conferences. If this model is successful, it may filter down to the lowest levels of the postseason, should those games survive at all.

6. Does the "amateur code" have any remaining vitality?

Of the NCAA's three major historical roles—creating and maintaining a national rulebook, negotiation of television contracts, and enforcement of amateurism standards—only its role in enforcing amateurism standards remains a significant facet of its operation. In fact, to most fans, the NCAA is seen only as a police body, turning up on campuses, interviewing players and coaches, thumbing through receipts for signs of malfeasance. The other functions of the organization have long since vanished, or are hidden from public view.

When the NCAA took over its role as guardian of amateurism in the 1950s, it was responding to public demand. The NCAA did not invent the amateur code, though it did help define how the concept would be operationalized in college sports. Nor did the NCAA force amateurism upon unwilling fans. It was the public backlash against the specter of professional athletes on campus that drove first the conferences to action, then later the NCAA.

This is no longer true. The thought of college players earning a regular paycheck from colleges no longer draws the public enmity it once did. In fact, public perception has swung the opposite direction. College sports have become big business, with college football alone a billion-dollar operation each season. At the same time, the players—the backbone of the entire affair—earn the same measly athletic scholarships they earned in the 1950s. If you ask the average fan, he is likely to claim that college football needs a whole lot less amateurism, not more of it.

Meanwhile, what was once a simple concept, at least in theory—college athletes should be amateurs—has spawned a labyrinthine code of regulations dense and complicated enough to make even the steeliest bureaucrat shudder. Teams are restricted in what spreads they can provide players should they offer morning bagels. Seemingly innocuous recruiting ploys, such as having high school athletes run onto the stadium field through smoke from a fog machine, are considered violations. Every football-playing college in America employs a compliance specialist—and at large schools, an entire compliance department—to ensure that these little rules are not broken. Even a full-time staff is not enough to prevent infractions completely, and each year every athletic department self-reports a handful of violations they unwittingly committed during the course of their affairs.

The connection between amateurism and these regulations is frayed. In fact, the NCAA's amateur code today makes more sense if we think of these rules as a means of leveling the playing field across colleges, and not as a way of maintaining athletic purity. Many schools cannot afford to pay players, no matter the level of payment. Should schools be permitted to pay athletes, a further divide would open between the haves and have-nots, severing the already tenuous connection between the members of Division I. Thought of this way, today's amateur code is no different than, say, the NFL salary cap; both devices are a means to ensure that as many teams remain as competitive as possible, in order to maximize fan interest.

If this is true, football programs and the NCAA must make a stark decision. Despite residing in the same division, a wide gulf in revenue and profitability exists between the top and bottom members of Division I-A. In the name of parity, thousands of players go without cost-of-living payments that their schools would gladly provide if only they were permitted under NCAA rules. The quixotic quest of certain small schools to play major college football has led not only to the bankrupting of athletic departments across America, but also to football players at economically healthy athletic departments not receiving a share of the multimillion dollar revenue they help drive each season.

7. Is professional minor league football a viable alternative?

The first football game ever played was between Princeton and Rutgers. College football predates the game at any other level. There has never been a time where professional football existed and college football did not. And since the earliest days of football, professional leagues have drawn upon the college ranks to replenish their rosters. This arrangement has worked quite well for both the NFL, which does not have to maintain (and pay for) minor league players, and the colleges, which have a monopoly over 18–22 year old talent.

Every now and again, a competitor to the NFL arises. The most successful of those leagues, the American Football League ("AFL"), became strong enough to force a merger with the NFL. Other leagues, most notably the United States Football League ("USFL") in the 1980s, have successfully encouraged top college players to forgo the NFL and play for the upstart league instead.

College football has not yet faced a challenge nearly as powerful as that presented even by the USFL, much less the AFL. This is peculiar at first blush. The NFL succeeds because it is football played at the very highest level of the sport. If there were a league called the PFL created tomorrow, and if the PFL somehow stole every one of the players away from the NFL and set up teams in each of the NFL cities, the PFL would become more popular than the NFL overnight. Of course, the PFL will have a tough time stealing away enough talent to be viable, since the NFL has built itself up into a multi-billion dollar organization and can offer more money to more players on almost every occasion.

One might think that a professional league would instead try convincing athletically gifted teenagers to forgo college and earn a paycheck for a few years before heading to the NFL. But unlike as against the NFL, if the PFL stole every player from every college roster tomorrow, there is at least a reasonable chance college football would still be more popular. This is because so much of the value in college football is tied up with the institutions, rather than the players. The NBA stole the top high school basketball players for years, yet college basketball never suffered for it. Nor is college basketball much better off now that the NBA no longer permits teams to draft high school players.

But this is all just supposition until we acquire direct evidence. The rival professional leagues have been kind enough to college football to install the same age requirements as the NFL. Someday, undoubtedly, a league will attempt to siphon off some of the talent currently stuck in college. We will learn very quickly to what extent schools, not players, provide the value in college football. If the answer is "less than we think," the result could render college football a niche sport like college baseball.

8. Is football safe?

Football's first crisis was about player safety. Football's final crisis may be as well. The high-profile suicides of Dave Duerson and Junior Seau have drawn public attention to the gruesome mental scars that football players carry after their careers have ended. We now know more—and understand better—the long-term effects of concussions and other brain trauma.

Professional, college, and high school football leaders are attempting to get in front of the issue. Tackles that fans would have applauded a generation ago draw penalties or even suspensions today. Progress is slow, but leaders at all levels of the game are trying to move away from the culture of big hits and rung bells that has defined football for so long.

Perhaps more worrisome than the massive blows to the head, however, is the accumulating evidence that the regular sub-concussive impact suffered by athletes on nearly every play may also contribute to brain deterioration over time. The Boston University School of Medicine has discovered chronic traumatic encephalopathy ("CTE")—a degenerative brain disease that correlates with depression, psychosis, and other neurological issues—in several deceased football players, including some that have not played the game beyond high school. Even if big hits are legislated out of the game, regular sub-concussive contact cannot be removed from football without fundamentally changing the sport. If the threat of CTE is unavoidable, many parents may no longer permit their children to play the sport. And should interest in football dry up at the lowest levels, the effects are certain to be felt everywhere in the game, up through college and the professional ranks.

To be sure, the medical evidence is still uncertain. CTE is difficult to diagnose during life, and many athletes who report no negative side effects have been diagnosed with the disease after death, so it is difficult to tell whether CTE is always harmful. As a whole, professional football players are healthier than non-football playing men at similar demographic levels. Athletes have played football for quite a long time, with most of those games played with far worse safety equipment and with far less concern for brain trauma. It would be peculiar if the threat of injury were worse today than it was two generations ago, and yet the vast majority of players from that era have lived their lives free from the symptoms associated with CTE.

Perception is reality, however, and a popular backlash against the sport may be beginning. Popular author Malcolm Gladwell has called for an abolition to college football, and an unknowable number of parents have kept their children away from the sport out of fear of brain injuries. Whether the fears of CTE are founded or not—and the science may take many, many years to develop—one can imagine fears about injuries capturing enough parents that child football disappears from many areas. Should the public come to see football participation as only a step or two removed from legalized child abuse, the sport is doomed at every level of play.

None of this is certain to happen. Fans of the early 20th century learned to shrug off serious injury and even death. It may be that, even if the threat of CTE is real, Americans are unable or unwilling to separate themselves from football entirely. Further rules changes and advances in technology may paper over medical dangers, just as the introduction of the forward pass helped soothe public concerns over safety despite not making the sport any safer than it previously had been. But there is a chance those safety concerns are not met on time, and that a generation of children who would have been raised playing and watching football will instead be shepherded into other sports. If this occurs, football may survive, but it will gradually shrivel in old age as future generations retain their childhood interests in lieu of football.

Unlike the other changes to the sport listed above, worries over safety present a mortal threat to college football. An expanded postseason, or reduction in the size of Division I-A, or even a decline in television revenue, will not kill football. Safety concerns might, even if that seems unlikely today. Dog fights were once reported in the sports sections of newspapers; the ongoing success of a pastime is by no means guaranteed. As such, leaders at all levels of football must take ownership of the safety issue and assure that everything possible is being done to guarantee the long-term health of participants. Many fans will grumble about the wussification of the game—just as many fans grumbled about "manliness" at the beginning of the 20th century—but we will adjust to the new football, just as we learned to love the forward pass.

Acknowledgements

Early while writing this book, I decided to forgo footnotes or in-text citations. My reason was simple: I did not want to scare readers away from what they might perceive as an academic work. In-text citation is a necessary evil; it detracts from the work stylistically, since citation invites hesitation and distraction as readers are tempted to jump from text to footnote to text. But readers also must have faith that what you are saying is *accurate,* and previous writers deserve credit for the work they have done to make the current project possible.

With those aims in mind, I will spend a few pages outlining the most helpful sources during this project. I should caution that it is not a complete list. The very most interesting sources, especially for older information, are contemporaneous newspaper records. A historian or even casual fan can learn much from simply reading the newspapers of the day. Dozens of hours were spent scrolling through microfilm, with no particular article in mind. Much of this time was fruitless, but even the hours that uncovered no useable material were helpful to me in absorbing the atmosphere of the time. There is no possible citation for that. And for the many hundreds of articles that were used, the vast majority of the citations would be unhelpful or unnecessary, since most were used merely to corroborate a date or place. If the reader doubts the veracity of these factual claims, then no doubt a quick internet search will confirm or dispel his suspicions without need for knowing which newspaper article from 1927 or 1902 I used to confirm the claim.

***

The single best academic history of college football—and perhaps the only modern academic history of college football—is John Sayle Watterson's *College Football: History, Spectacle, Controversy* (Johns Hopkins University Press, 2000). If the reader, following the end of this book, would like a more thorough accounting of the sport's history, without the emphasis on the formation and interaction of the conferences, Watterson's in-depth work is the place to look. Also, for the researcher, Watterson's list of references is an invaluable jumping-off point.

When I began writing, there was no helpful account on the rules crisis of the early 20th century. That gap, quite thankfully, was filled by John J. Miller's *The Big Scrum: How Teddy Roosevelt Saved Football* (Harper 2011). Miller's conclusions are not my own, and I disagree with his narrative in some important respects, but he has done a great service in writing about a chapter of college football's history that previously had been shrouded in mythology.

Regarding the CFA-NCAA struggle over television contracts, there is no substitute for the briefs and opinions that came about from the litigation. To the extent that background was needed to illuminate gaps, several interviews were conducted with many of the major participants from that struggle. Apart from those primary sources, Professor John Siegfried wrote a short history of the College Football Association in his article "The College Football Association Television Broadcast Cartel" (The Antitrust Bulletin, Fall 2004, 799–819). Finally, if the reader is interested in learning more about antitrust law generally, I highly suggest Herbert Hovenkamp's *The Antitrust Enterprise: Principle and Execution* (Harvard University Press 2008 [2nd edition]), as I found myself returning to that book several times to ensure I was not mucking up the legal analysis.

Two sources were particularly illuminating with regards to the Southwest Conference. Paul Burka wrote an eerily prescient article entitled "The Decline and Fall of the Southwest Conference" for the September 1974 edition of *Texas Monthly*; it took another two decades for the SWC to disband, but Burka accurately diagnosed the maladies that would eventually kill the conference. The second major source was David Whitford's *A Payroll to Meet: A Story of Greed, Corruption, and Football at SMU* (Collier 1989). It remains the single best source for information on the SMU football scandal to this day. Regarding the scandals of the era in general, Don Yaeger's *Undue Process: The NCAA's Injustice for All* (Sagamore 1991) is—despite its overwrought tone and reliance on anonymous sourcing—a helpful guide to the scandals and procedures of the 1970s and 1980s.

Regarding Notre Dame's early history and rivalry with Michigan, two sources stand out. The first, John Kryk's *Natural Enemies: The Notre Dame-Michigan Football Feud* (Andrews Mcmeel 1994), provides a rather balanced look at the various tussles between Fielding Yost and Knute Rockne. The second, Murray Sperber's *Shake Down the Thunder: The Creation of Notre Dame Football* (Indiana University Press 2002) is more pro-Notre Dame, but not stiflingly so. Edward Sorin, founder of Notre Dame, also left behind his chronicles, which Arthur J. Hope used as the foundation of his celebratory history of the school, entitled *Notre Dame – First 100 Years*. Both sources are made freely available in Notre Dame's online archives.

As the narrative approaches the modern day, this work becomes even less dependent upon books and more dependent upon interviews. There are a few books from this era worth reading, not so much because I used them as sources (though they did undoubtedly influence my thinking), but instead because they are simply valuable in their own rights. Stewart Mandel's *Bowls, Polls, and Tattered Souls: Tackling the Chaos and Controversy that Reign over College Football* (Wiley 2007) is a sarcastic, well-written look at the various intrigues that surround modern college football. Michael Oriard, a former college and professional football player and today a professor at Oregon State University, has written a history of modern college football—*Bowled Over: Big-Time College Football from the Sixties to the BCS Era* (University of North Carolina Press 2009)—that drastically differs in emphasis from this book. Oriard focuses on the racial integration of the sport in the late 1960s and early 1970s, and then later turns his attention to debates over academic standards. Neither topic has received much attention in my own work, and I disagree with a great many of Mr. Oriard's conclusions, but his book is nevertheless recommended.

Despite my aforementioned policy of not stopping to mention each and every newspaper article scanned during the research for this book, a few articles (and writers) deserve credit for substantially adding to our understanding of college football's recent history. Mark Blaudschun of the Boston Globe chronicled Boston College's entry into the ACC in his June 30, 2005 article "BC's Bumpy Landing." More recently, Teddy Greenstein wrote in the July 1, 2011 Chicago Tribune about the failed ESPN-Big Ten negotiations in 2004 that eventually led to the creation of the Big Ten Network and all that followed.

***

This project has consumed over two years, undergone countless revisions and reformulations, and caused countless sleepless nights. After so much time and energy, I am excited to be done, but also saddened. No longer can I turn on my computer on a lazy Tuesday night and begin fiddling with syntax or searching for that one source that I know must exist somewhere. Like all books, this work is flawed, and despite the contributions of so many, those flaws are entirely of my own doing. That is the ultimate disappointment of the author. And yet I've learned, at some point, we must let go. I can only hope that my contributions outweigh the imperfections, and I trust I will find some other way to fill my evenings in the future.

About the Author

Steven Donohue (born 1986)—a native of Chicago, Illinois—earned his bachelor's degree from the University of Illinois at Urbana-Champaign in 2008. While at Illinois, he was awarded the Robert H. Bierma award for excellence in undergraduate scholarship by the College of Liberal Arts and Sciences. Donohue earned his law degree from the University of Chicago in 2011, where he participated on the *University of Chicago Law Review* and graduated with honors. He currently resides in Minneapolis, Minnesota with his wife Alison and three adorable cats.

Made in the USA
Lexington, KY
02 July 2013